JAMES HALLIDAY

A Life in Wine

James Halliday -

JAMES
HALLIDAY
A Life in Wine

hardie grant books
MELBOURNE · LONDON

Published in 2012 by Hardie Grant Books

Hardie Grant Books (Australia)
Ground Floor, Building 1
658 Church Street
Richmond, Victoria 3121
www.hardiegrant.com.au

Hardie Grant Books (UK)
Dudley House, North Suite
34–35 Southampton Street
London WC2E 7HF
www.hardiegrant.co.uk

Cataloguing-in-Publication data is available from the National Library of Australia.

A Life in Wine

ISBN 9781740666725

Cover design by Philip Campbell Design
Text design by Philip Campbell Design
Typesetting by Philip Campbell Design
Typeset in Adobe Garamond Premier Pro 11.75/16pt
Colour reproduction by Splitting Image Colour Studio
Printed and bound in China by 1010 Printing International Limited

Dedicated to the memory of
Len Evans AO OBE

TABLE OF CONTENTS

Preface   1

CHAPTER 1: In the Beginning   13

CHAPTER 2: Early Days   25

CHAPTER 3: 1962: A Short Intermission   37

CHAPTER 4: 1963–68: The Accumulation   49

CHAPTER 5: It Gets Serious 1969–70   59

CHAPTER 6: Brokenwood 1970–83   71

CHAPTER 7: Bulletin Place 1969–83   91

CHAPTER 8: European Sojourns 1979–85   113

CHAPTER 9: Signs of Things to Come 1975–85   129

CHAPTER 10: Dual Residence 1983–88   137

CHAPTER 11: Coldstream Hills 1988–96   159

CHAPTER 12: Wine Tastings Over the Decades   193

CHAPTER 13: The Flight of Icarus 1985–2010   205

CHAPTER 14: The Len Evans Memorial Tutorials   219

CHAPTER 15: The Single Bottle Club Dinners: A Reprise   231

CHAPTER 16: Farewell   251

Acknowledgements   263

PREFACE

On 16 August 2006 my world changed forever. The night before, I and several other mutual friends had dinner with Len Evans at the family house, Loggerheads, in the Hunter Valley. As normal, generous amounts of very good wine were consumed, and the dinner was far from over when I announced that I simply had to go to bed, because I had to drive back to Sydney early the following morning to catch a plane to New Zealand.

As always with my trips to the Hunter, it was obligatory that I stayed at Loggerheads (the name Len and Trish had come up with for their house), and I left the following morning before Len had arisen. He was due to drive to Newcastle later in the day with daughter Jodie to collect Trish from hospital (she was undergoing ongoing treatment after the removal of a cancerous tumour from her breast), so I had no desire to disturb him.

Some months previously Len had had a newly developed pacemaker implanted. For several years prior to this he had had serious health problems stemming from bypass surgery in 1988, and it was tacitly accepted that it was highly likely that he would predecease Trish. I would ring him at least once a week, partly to discuss the outcome of cricket Test matches, rugby union internationals, or golf tournaments, but also to check on his health.

I fully understood that after the bypass surgery Len had considered his heart specialist's ultimatum that he must change his lifestyle

---

OPPOSITE: *Len Evans and author, circa 2000. We were always ready for a laugh.*

1

– moderate his wine consumption, eat less and travel less – and decided that a short, happy life was infinitely preferable to a long, miserable one. So I left any admonishments to Trish.

The new pacemaker had in fact worked miracles. Fluid accumulation in his chest reduced dramatically, and his physical energy was equally increased. Suddenly it seemed possible that he would outlive Trish, and his close friends and I started to worry about the cost – the feasibility, even – of funding wines for his 80th birthday that would match, let alone exceed, those we had assembled for his 75th birthday in 2005.

It was with these thoughts that I landed in New Zealand with a group of wine journalists to attend a Test between the Wallabies and the All Blacks (and a wine programme put together by Montana Wines, aka Brancott Estate). The organiser was Stuart Gregor, a consummate PR operator in the wine arena, and a long-term friend, who had arrived earlier.

He walked toward me with none of his usual bonhomie, and even before he began to speak, I knew something was dreadfully wrong. Nonetheless, I was totally unprepared for his words 'James, I'm so sorry, but Len's dead.' I wanted to say 'He can't be, I was with him last night', but no words of any kind formed on my lips.

What started as a friendship 35 years earlier had grown into something much more than that, transcending respect and morphing into unconditional love. Looking back, I'm not sure precisely how long it took, nor whether there was any particular event that caused me to realise how deep our bonds were. But it was most certainly not his death that belatedly triggered recognition of my love for him, and of his for me.

Len was a man of extraordinary generosity, never counting the cost, which was for many years beyond his financial capacity. He was highly intelligent, fiercely loyal to his friends, contemptuous of sycophants. His sense of humour was second to none; he was a great MC and a fearsome auctioneer when raising money for charities; and gave hilarious after-dinner speeches when the mood took him.

Each time I arrived at Loggerheads for a stay, the family dachshunds would bark in a frenzy (not because they recognised me, but because they were dachshunds) and I knew that by the time I got out of my car, Len would have appeared from the house, smiling and saying, 'My dear chap, how are you?' and would go on to tell me which room I would be staying in. It was a ritual that stretched back to 1985. It had been repeated countless times, but had never lost its meaning.

Loggerheads has now been sold, and I would never wish to return – it would simply be too painful. But it does provide me still with many wonderful memories, going back to the time it was built – on the top of a hill with a spectacular vista, the backdrop provided by the stark outline of the Brokenback Range, deepening purple as the sun set behind it, flaring in resentment as it slid below the Range.

It was built in the form of a squared U, the two arms separated at the base by the very large living room, kitchen and dining room. One side of the U, slightly smaller than the other, was occupied by the family, including their three children – Sally, Jodie and Toby – until they moved on, to return periodically, of course, ultimately with grandchildren.

The other side of the U had four large rooms, with a roofed but otherwise open paved passage leading back to the main living area, flanking the croquet lawn, the half-tennis court and the first tee of the five-hole golf course. It was this passage that caused great grief during the building approval process. Cessnock Council insisted that it be totally enclosed in accordance with its home building

code. 'But how is it that motels offer even less access cover for their rooms?' expostulated Len. 'Ah, if you were building a motel there would be no problem,' came the answer.

'Well, what do I have to do to get permission to build a motel?' Len responded. 'You have to get permission from the County of Cumberland.' Application made and fees paid, the County bureaucrat indicated that approval would be given subject to proof of adequate off-street parking. The street – Palmers Lane – was well over 100 metres from the house, and the whole property was over 100 hectares in size. After a moment's thought, Len replied, 'There is room for 20 buses, 200 cars and 500 motorcycles. Is that enough?'

Approval to build a motel given, construction began in earnest, and a casual observer might well have concluded that this was indeed a large motel, if not a Maharajah's palace. Len was a life-long bowerbird, but not just of small things. Before Loggerheads was even a twinkle in his eye he had acquired massive beams retrieved from a dismantled Sydney wharf built 100 years or so previously, a large Spanish castle door, and a collection of very old English oak furniture. When the time came for the beams to be brought to the Hunter from Sydney, Len could not resist the temptation to have them dragged by a bullock team for the last part of the journey.

Numerous trips to English and Australian antique shops had yielded a collection of objects to go on walls and tables, ancient toilets with amazing plumbing systems, a collection of antiquarian books selected for their bizarre titles, and many more such things. Each guest room had its own name and theme, and was filled with antiques, some valuable, some simply quirky.

He was also architect and head building contractor for the house, co-opting all and sundry to assist in its construction, bagging walls and laying large tiles, some made by himself (he installed his own kiln), some by others. Some were delivered by truck. On one truck delivery, with the house virtually built, the truckie was accompanied by his wife. Len delighted in recounting the conversation with her that followed: 'Why, Mr Evans, what you are doing here is so wonderful.' 'Thank you.' 'It must have been so much work.' 'Yes, indeed.' 'Why, Mr Evans, anyone else would simply have let it fall down.'

As well as a potter, he was a sculptor, not only of small things, but of large things, some very large. He created a masterpiece at Hugh Johnson's property on the Dordogne, using power tools to sculpt the stone, which was then seated on a large concrete foundation sunk into the soil. It, quite literally, very nearly killed him, for he ingested stone dust that accumulated in his chest. When Hugh Johnson sold the property a few years later, he baulked at the idea of endeavouring to extract and return the sculpture (which he had not commissioned) to his home in Essex. Len was mortally offended by the decision, the practical difficulties notwithstanding.

He was, however, not offended when he proudly showed Anders Ousbach (himself a self-taught artist and sculptor of exceptional skill) the latest of his numerous sandstone works of art that were dotted through the grass, shrubs and trees on the right-hand side of the last 50 or so metres of the road leading to the house. Ousbach slowly and silently walked around the sculpture one way, then turned around and circumnavigated it the other way. 'Well,' he eventually said, 'there it is.' It was a story Len loved to tell.

He built a large sandstone tableau inlaid with coloured ceramics dedicated to Suzanne and me, with allegorical references (so he said) to aspects of my character – for once, complimentary, for like most Australian males, we delighted in teasing each other. The plinth stands at the front of our garden, fronting the parking area of our house at Coldstream Hills, and I hope it will always have a home.

Part of our friendship was built upon the competitive nature of our personalities. As I told friends at the time (in the early 1970s), I played a game of squash with Len, taking the first two games 9–1 and 9–2, before losing in five games. Around the same time I gave him fly-casting lessons in the back garden of his then house in Greenwich, as together with David Bright (lifelong friend and merchant banker), Michael Hornibrook (best man at my first wedding), Andrew Clayton (senior partner Clayton Utz), Vic Kelly (lawyer, wine lover, poker player), Jason Garrett (creator of the London Lakes Fly Fishing Resort in the highlands of Tasmania), Don Francois (then Director of Fisheries in New South Wales but also the owner and winemaker for his eponymous Chateau Francois vineyard and winery in the Hunter Valley) we had a long weekend's

A Life in Wine

The sandstone and ceramic plinth made by Len Evans for the author and his wife, complete with allegorical messages.

trout fishing planned on a property on the Kybean River, in the Monaro.

We arrived the day before Len, and caught a large number of fish. He arrived that night, and despite a seven-card stud poker game played well past midnight, was like a cat on a hot tin roof early the following morning, badgering me to take him down to the river. At the head of the first pool we came to, a trout was rising. It was a considerable distance upstream, and I knew it was well beyond his casting capacity. After some fruitless attempts, I said 'Here, let me show you how', figuring that it would be useful for him to see how you have to strike if the fish takes the fly, and how to play it and land it.

I duly caught the fish, and for years thereafter Len would tell how I elbowed him out of the way, and stole what would have been his first trout. I went back to the house for breakfast, realising my presence wasn't wanted, and an hour or so later he did in fact catch a fish, and brought it back in triumph to the house. It was admired, photographed, put in a freezer bag to take back to Sydney, exhumed for further admiration, until we suggested that Evans might cook it for his breakfast (it wasn't much over the legal minimum), we having already had ours.

He agreed, and deglazed one of the two electric frying pans we had used for our breakfast by opening a bottle of champagne and adding butter, removing the trout when largely cooked, placing it in the second pan while reducing the sauce further, then returning the trout for the finishing touches. All was ready when he spied some juice from the fish in the second pan, and added it to his trout as the final touch. Unfortunately, the 'juice' was concentrated lemon Fab, which frothed mightily on being added.

The tragedy was of such magnitude that we were (just) able to conceal our mirth as the remainder of the champagne was used in an attempt to get rid of the soap. We never learnt how successful it was, for we were not offered, no did we ask for, part of his trout, but I cannot imagine that all taste of the washing up liquid was removed.

Much of what follows in this book was in fact written prior to Len's death. It is the only time I have embarked on a book without finishing it in one hit, but other works came up that I considered more important. So I was left with a major problem: rewrite the book entirely, or leave it intact. I have chosen the latter course, but doing so makes the anachronisms all the more obvious, for I bring this chapter to a close by jumping to the Single Bottle Club Dinner held on 9 September 2005, to celebrate his 75th birthday.

I recount later the history of the Single Bottle Club dinners, and how they were created and paid for. Suffice it to say now that the 2005 celebration was unique: we agreed that we would procure all the wines and simply tell Len that we had no need of his help in any way, shape or form. He was born on 31 August 1930, a dreadful vintage across the length and breadth of Europe. By contrast, 1929 was a very great vintage, and it was the year of his conception. So most of the wines came from that vintage, the centrepiece being a magnum of 1929 Romanée-Conti (from the Domaine de la Romanée-Conti, of course) purchased for a very large sum of money from a Belgian cellar.

I was the policeman, constantly in fear that someone might let slip what the theme of the dinner was, and, worse still, the vinous centrepiece. If he knew in advance what wines were to be served that night, he was a consummate actor, but I am certain he didn't. It was a wonderful night, and while I have always been hopelessly remiss in retaining keepsakes, I did keep the letter he wrote to me.

Sept 16th 2005

My dear James,

I've been struggling for some days with this letter since I don't really know what to say. How can one thank you enough for all you did for that most magnificent dinner? It was truly remarkable, never to be repeated, and I do realise the trouble to which you went to make it all possible. Obviously there were outstanding wines and the mounting tension of quality gave great style to the evening. But what a wine to lead to! Quite the most magnificent Burgundy I've ever had, though I have had older R.C.s with Lalou years ago. I understand it cost a fortune. Thank heavens I only cost a 1/15th of the fortune spent. You realise, of course, that this makes the future dinners and your celebrations (2008) difficult to do. There's no way that dinner could ever be topped. You and I will have to talk about getting down to some kind of basics.

Whatever, it was a glory, and I thank you from the bottom (actually, not the good bit) of my much damaged and much used heart for making it one of the great evenings of my life – certainly the greatest wine dinner.

It is dribbling with rain, which is comforting in every way, we finished up with 100 applicants (still coming in) [for the Tutorial]. You've been sent the list for examination. Do let us try to get a little time together to discuss the future.

Well, old chap, you'll go down in some form of history. I am looking forward with great delight to sending the lists to all.

All love, Len

CHAPTER 1

IN THE BEGINNING

My introduction to wine began in the years immediately following the Second World War. My father John was a physician – a heart specialist – and had spent the war years in the Australian Army, serving mainly in the Middle East, rising to the rank of Colonel by the time he was discharged.

Since I had been born in 1938, and my mother (Muriel), brother (Peter) and sister (Janet) had moved to the safety of our second house at Moss Vale, I barely saw my father until the conclusion of the war.

I was also an afterthought. Peter had been born in 1926, Janet following in 1928, whereafter the family moved to England while my father studied for and obtained his FRCP (Fellow of the Royal College of Physicians) postgraduate degree. Among other things,

OPPOSITE: *A very reluctant portrait sitter, aged 10 or 11.*

my parents were exposed to good French wine while there. When they returned to Australia and purchased a house at 123 Victoria Road, Bellevue Hill, they made several key alterations.

One was to literally jack up a generous quarter of the house, which had uninterrupted views of Rose Bay and out to the Sydney Heads. The purpose was to take advantage of the slope of the site (which plunged vertically beyond the front stone wall boundary) and create a large downstairs bedroom plus bathroom, and a stone-walled, walk-in wine cellar.

The downstairs bedroom was occupied by my brother, and – much later – by myself. Apart from a few miscellaneous bottles of other provenance (particularly dry sherry and brandy), the wooden racks of the cellar were filled with Rieslings, Hocks, Chablis, White Burgundies, Red Burgundies and Clarets, all with bin numbers as part of their label identification.

They were, in fact, all Lindeman wines, all made in the Hunter Valley. When, 15 years or so later, I told my father that all the white wines had been made from semillon (with slightly different picking dates) and all the red wines from hermitage (as it was always called then in the Hunter), he was surprised and slightly bemused. What did it matter, he wondered; he knew how each wine should taste, and knew that some of the bins (Private Bins in those days: Reserve Bins were a thing of the future) were better than others – primeval vintage variation at work.

From the time he returned from England he had become a valued private trade customer of Lindemans. It was in receivership, Leo Buring having been appointed to that role by the Commercial Banking Company of Sydney, but was continuing to trade as normal from its Sydney headquarters in the basement of the Queen Victoria Building; Penfolds was its co-tenant in another part of the basement.

A Life in Wine

T he wine industry of the 1940s operated in a strange environment. The focus on fortified wine continued as it had for the prior 40 years, but while it suffered from war-time shortages (no new bottles were made, corks were routinely cut in half and so forth), it benefited greatly from strict beer rationing. While this technically ended on 27 December 1945, beer remained in chronically short supply until the end of the 1940s, and fortified wine (notably cream sherry) and brandy were the obvious alternatives. Equally strange was the distribution system: wineries in New South Wales had to be members of the Wine and Brandy Producers Association, which then negotiated prices with the breweries, which in turn owned the hotels through which wine was sold. Not only were prices absolutely fixed, but it was easier to negotiate price rises than reductions, because the hoteliers received a set percentage of the retail price. It was a decade of prosperity, and as import controls of raw materials were eased in the second half, of significant growth.

Given that upwards of 90 per cent of all Australian sales were of fortified wines, and given the receivership of Lindemans, the exalted social status which all doctors held at that time, and the fact that he typically purchased five cases or more on each visit to Lindemans, it is not surprising that my father was accorded the red carpet treatment. Nor did Lindemans' emergence from receivership in 1947 alter things. When, ten years or so later, I accompanied him to Lindemans' new premises at Nyrang Street, Lidcombe, it was still like a state visit.

There I met Ray Kidd, who had succeeded Bert Bear as general manager, and Gerry Sissingh, a youthful Dutchman who had worked at Chateau Cos d'Estournel before coming to Australia. Our paths were to cross many times in the future, but I had no way of guessing that at the time. They were an odd couple: Kidd, slim, quietly spoken and pedantic in the extreme, and Sissingh, as solid and four-square as the proverbial brick outhouse, and loudly spoken.

When, in the 1970s, I wrote that Lindemans Ben Ean Moselle (then the number one white wine in Australia) no longer contained any wine from Lindemans' Ben Ean vineyards, Kidd took me to task, saying I was incorrect. When I protested, 'But Ray, all the grapes from Ben Ean go to your top Hunter Valley wines,' he replied, 'Yes, that's true, but we have the white wine pressings to dispose of, and they go into Ben Ean.' 'How much do they represent – half a per cent?' I responded, gaining a barely perceptible nod of assent from Kidd.

Less still did I know in the latter part of the 1940s, when I was appointed a semi-official butler at home, where I might one day end up. When we were to have wine – which was by no means every day – I would be told what was required, and it would be my job to fetch the bottle from the cellar.

Whenever wine was served, I was given a small glass. I maintain that it was diluted with water, something which in later years my father denied when I discussed it with him. The truth may be that in my younger years it was so diluted, and that when I became an early teenager, it was no longer watered down. Either way, I became accustomed to its taste.

Two particular incidents remain permanently imprinted on my mind. My brother Peter was then a medical student at Sydney University, and was dissecting a stingray which had been inadequately preserved in formalin. The stench was nauseating; the dissection seemed to go on forever, and to this day I have no idea how he put up with it.

While it briefly made the cellar trips less than enjoyable, one occasion in 1949 was on another scale altogether. It was during the coal miners' strike, which led to blackouts across Sydney at all times of day and night until Prime Minister Ben Chifley called in the army to break the strike.

As often happened, we were without electricity, but since my mother (an excellent cook) had a gas stove, it did not interfere with dinner, and I was sent down, armed with a candle, to collect a particularly precious bottle. As I turned to leave the cellar, candle in one hand, bottle in the other, the candle was blown out, and a combined skeleton and ghost, wailing with a high-pitched sound, an eerie light coming from its eyes, sought to grab hold of me.

Needless to say, I was paralysed with terror, and dropped the bottle on the concrete floor, with predictable results. My screams brought parental aid, and the unmasking of my brother, who had wrapped himself in a white sheet, and put a small torch inside the head of the skeleton he had on loan from the university as another part of his medical studies.

In 1952, aged 13, I was consigned as a boarder to Cranbrook School, also in Victoria Road. I had previously been a day boy. Since I had been born at a private hospital almost diagonally opposite our house, I ended up with the unusual distinction of having been born in, lived in, and gone to boarding school in the same street.

In that first year as a boarder I was repeatedly sent to sickbay suffering from colds or flu, and was taken to my ear, nose and throat specialist uncle Sir George Halliday's rooms in Macquarie Street. He removed a number of polyps from my left nostril (without the benefit of anaesthetic) and I was brought home after a precaution-ary x-ray. I was woken early next morning to be told I was going to Royal Prince Alfred Hospital where Uncle George was going to per-form another operation, this time under ether anaesthetic. He was due to fly to the United States later that morning, and I was told he was taken to the airport at high speed by a police escort to catch his plane. Nonetheless, I was less than impressed when a week or so later a nursing sister removed what seemed to be an amazing amount of tape from the upper recesses of my nose. Why, I wondered in my childish way, hadn't he done that himself? I was told at the time that some bone had been removed from the area behind and to the right of my eye, and I wouldn't be able to continue playing contact sport. What I didn't learn until many years later was that a malignant can-cerous growth had been removed; in the meantime, repeated visits to Uncle George's rooms involved scraping away at the site of the excavation, a precautionary measure (I ultimately learnt); I was one of the lucky few.

Prior to boarding school, my term reports had been the cause of much lecturing and recriminations by my father, who (along with his 12 brothers and sisters) had excelled academically, as had my sis-ter and brother. I invariably came in the bottom quarter of most subjects, with a chorus of teachers commenting on my disruptive behaviour and refusal to apply myself.

In my defence, I would add that I was forced to do Latin, French, Physics and Mathematics, all of which I detested, and my results in English and History were at the other end of the scale. Moreover, I had known I was not going to follow in the medical footsteps of my father, uncles, brother and cousins since the night I was in the

---

OPPOSITE: *Brokenwood Graveyard Vineyard – the source of its eponymous icon Shiraz.*

A Life in Wine

kitchen watching my mother cook when she sliced off the ball of her thumb with a bread knife, so most of my subjects seemed irrelevant.

In retrospect, I made one major error during my first year as a boarder. I became involved in a year-long battle with my would-be French teacher, resulting in my spending prolonged periods standing in the corner of the classroom with one handkerchief stuffed in my mouth and another wrapped around my head, holding the gag in place. What I failed to appreciate was my teacher's Rhodes Scholarship, his Rugby Union Blue from Oxford University, and his strength of character – he become headmaster of Shore School some years later. 'Jaika' Travers was not a man to be trifled with.

Obviously enough, I very much regret the lost opportunity to gain a background of French. However, I read voraciously, and had a brilliant English teacher, C.A. 'Cheery' Bell (he seldom smiled). Nonetheless, my school days overall were far from happy, and my diligence as a student did not increase as a consequence of becoming a boarder.

When I was let out on day leave on Sunday in my later years as a boarder I would walk home to an empty house, as my parents spent many weekends at Moss Vale. I made use of the house with my first serious girlfriend, but those were the days of innocence. We would get into bed naked, kiss passionately, but that was all. Fear of pregnancy, I suppose, was why things did not progress, although they ultimately did some years later, in the far less accommodating surroundings of the front seat of a Morris Minor.

Nor can I explain why I at no time thought of borrowing a bottle of wine from the cellar, which also might have changed the Sunday trysts. Even smoking held no pleasure: I tried once or twice, decided I didn't like cigarettes, and that was that. Since drugs were not even on the horizon, it was an uneventful childhood and adolescence.

A Life in Wine

I suppose I should add that school holidays were an entirely different matter. I spent the second term holidays at a Border Leicester sheep stud called Warrambone, some miles from Gulargambone, where I learnt to ride and to shoot. The downside of this was the necessity of flying from Sydney to Dubbo in a DC3, then from Dubbo to Toorooweenah in a light plane, and thence to Gulargambone by car. Car, sea and aeroplane travel all had the same disastrous consequences. Indeed, by the time I made my second flight to Dubbo, a Pavlovian response to the sight of the DC3 caused me to start vomiting by the time I made it to the stairs, which produced an understandably wild-eyed response from the hostess and crinkled, disapproving noses from my fellow passengers.

The Christmas holidays were spent in my grandmother's house in Pacific Road, Palm Beach. Endless days were spent body surfing and fishing; there was a path of sorts winding more or less directly downhill, ending in a grove of palm trees that exited at the beach. It was a quick trip down, slower on the way up, especially the day I was carrying a five-foot shark slung over my shoulder; it had been caught in fishermen's nets. (In those far-off days, commercial fishing in hand-hauled nets still occurred at the protected end of the beach near the ocean swimming pool.)

The hand I had in the shark's mouth and the shoulder over which it had been draped were the worse for wear, but my grand plan remained – so I thought – intact. It was to cut the head off, and boil it to soften the flesh (to be fed to the chooks), leaving me with the shark's jaws as a memento. Alas, they turned to gelatine, my plan to ashes.

I slept in one of two beds on an open verandah-like room, protected by mosquito nets. At night, the sound of the waves crashing on the beach far below lulled me to sleep, with the occasional movements of the koalas in the large salmon-hued angophora trees only a few metres away also impinging on my consciousness.

In the early morning the beautiful cry of the currawongs always drew me from my slumber. To this day, the currawong's call instantly transports me back 60-plus years.

Looking back, holidays apart, I had a difficult childhood. It was not until I was approaching 40 that a reasonably relaxed relationship with my father was forged – the stubborn gene of the Halliday family was recognised by many.

On the other hand, I adored my mother, even if she on one occasion grabbed a flat plank of wood and whacked me several times hard across my thigh. Highly coloured bruises developed, and we agreed that I looked like a parrot fish. In the 1950s she described the huge American cars of the time with high tailfins as being 'By sea monster out of double bed.' Such sense of humour as I have was inherited from her, not from my father.

CHAPTER 2

EARLY DAYS

In 1956 I became a resident of St Paul's College, University of Sydney, embarking on an Arts degree with the option of either Architecture or Law to follow. I had obtained a Commonwealth Scholarship (liberally awarded in those days), and was still thoroughly undecided which way I wished to head once finished with university. After two years of Arts, I had the further option of undertaking a combined Arts/Law third year; since I would need to do this year whether I then switched to Architecture (another five years) or continued with Law (another three years), I was able to postpone the decision until the commencement of the 1959 academic year.

In the meantime I spent the maximum amount of time enjoying myself, and the minimum needed to scrape through the end of year examinations. At least I knew the subjects I was meant to be

OPPOSITE: *In the St Paul's College .303 rifle shooting team.*

studying, unlike one of my college friends who was doing a strange five-year Law course, and had to confess – when cornered by a college tutor – that at the start of third term he wasn't sure exactly which subjects he was enrolled in.

It wasn't that his social life interfered too much: nicknamed the Social Lion (on the red-haired bloke called Blue principle), he listened to classical music for much of the time, using an interesting three-field-fallow system for his shirts, socks, underpants, etc. These were consigned to a corner of his room, and would be rummaged through each morning (if he indeed arose in the morning) to find the least obviously dirty set to wear that day.

I filled the days with various pursuits: endless hours on the billiards tables resulted in my becoming college billiards champion, and one year, intercollegiate champion. (I refuse on principle to play these days because it is so embarrassing to miss shots I could achieve with my eyes closed 50 years ago.) I became a proficient ping pong player, a competent (and very fit) squash player, I shot .303 rifles for college, for Sydney University and (one year) in the Imperial Inter-Varsity competition.

I became a good bridge player, building on my education at home before going to university, and building on this with late-night sessions and (when I became an articled law clerk) lunchtime sessions. I did not reach the competition level of my best friend, Michael Hornibrook, but I could hold my own with all but the better competition players.

Poker, too, entered the scene; it alone endures to this day, although the opportunities are scarce. It was to become seriously financially rewarding in the 1970s, and helped pay for a substantial part of the wine cellar I was building up – more of which anon. All the other skills have vanished, partly through lack of practice, partly through the erosion of age.

I also sought, with mixed success, to become acquainted with as many residents as possible of the adjacent Women's College and the nearby Nurses Home of Royal Prince Alfred Hospital. These efforts gave rise to some unusual situations – such as the time I was locked in my room with a newly found friend by a system of ropes which prevented me from opening the door.

We were not overly concerned, until nature started to remind us that we had respectively consumed considerable amounts of alcohol earlier that evening. My room was on an upper floor of a building built in the 19th century, with narrow casement windows. It was simple enough for me to resolve my problem, but far more difficult for my friend. After various approaches, a sideways trapeze-like stance, one leg in, one out, with me holding one hand, brought her relief. All was dark outside (and we had turned the lights out), so the unusual sight was not shared with anyone.

Wine, too, became of increasing interest. On arrival, I disc-overed that the college had a formal wine cellar, run as a co-operative. It had wines from other makers, notably Penfolds and Tulloch, so my wine horizons were expanded overnight. In those days, black academic gowns were required to be worn on week-night evenings, and we were allowed to have wine on Wednesday evening and Sunday lunch. The food, it must be said, was Dickensian. Often the long-serving matron would address the table: 'Beef or lamb. Beef's off; what will you have?' I had come from four years of boarding school, where the acme of gastronomic pleasure was the Bonox gravy and slices of white bread, so there was no culture shock.

Even more important, the Wine Club made weekend day trips to the Hunter Valley. They were arranged through Johnny Walker of the Angus Steak Cave and Harry Brown of Rhinecastle Wines, the distributor of Tulloch Wines in New South Wales. So it was that we would go to Tulloch, where we sat at a rudimentary table on the earth floor of the galvanised shed winery while steaks of gargantuan proportion were barbecued for us.

I have the clearest memory of being plied with the 1954 Dry Red and the '54 Private Bin Dry Red. The '54 Private Bin secured fame by being awarded first prize in both the Claret and Burgundy classes in the same year at the Royal Sydney Wine Show. It caused a scandal, not because the same wine had been entered twice (in those days there was no rule prohibiting it, as there is today), but because Claret was meant to be a different style from Burgundy, and vice versa. Thus the judges' failure to reward one bottle and not the other was the problem.

At this time – the second half of the 1950s – the only accessible wineries were Tulloch (and then only because of our prior intro-duction through Rhinecastle) and Elliott's, which had a shop/cellar door in Cessnock. Lindemans, Draytons and McWilliam's were not open to the public, and Tyrrell's was then selling all its wine in bulk. There the options ended.

But nonetheless a group of friends – including the Social Lion and Tony Albert (also at St Paul's College, and later one of the three founders of Brokenwood, along with John Beeston and myself, but a year behind me) – made separate forays to the Hunter. We trav-elled the only viable way, leaving the Pacific Highway at Mangrove Mountain, and negotiating the rutted, twisting dirt road (little more than a track) which emerged at Wollombi. Upkeep on the convict-built road was desultory, to say the least, leading to the disintegration

A Life in Wine

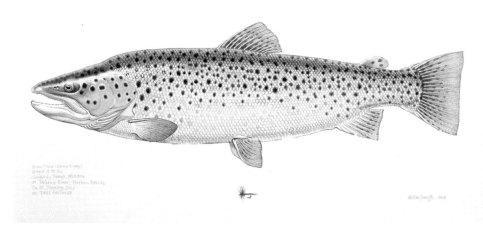

*A 5.75 lb brown trout caught by author at Mohaka River, Poronui
Ranch N.Z., on a Dad's Favourite fly on 28 January 2003.*

---

of the gear stick in one of my fellow Paulines' Volkswagen on one
trip home. We were sufficiently lubricated with wine to regard the
situation as highly amusing, a view not shared by the car's owner,
but we jury-rigged a means of getting back to Sydney.

A customary stop on the way to the Hunter was at the convict
drinking trough, a basin-like affair carved out of sandstone sitting on
the high side of the road (on the right-hand side travelling towards
Wollombi). The fact that it seldom held water was immaterial: we
stopped for a can (or two) of beer; it was Len Evans who pioneered
the opening of a bottle of Champagne, and for an archaeological-
like midden of champagne corks to accumulate. I was to follow suit
in the 1960s, whether or not in Len's company.

The wine industry of the 1950s was every bit as mixed up as I was. Domestic sales were falling, and by the end of the decade imports were increasing. The viticultural atlas was static at best, centred on the hot Riverland regions purpose-built for the production of the fortified wines which, with the restrictive hand of the beer industry and its tied hotels, counted for 80 to 90 per cent of the market.

Beneath the surface, however, the seeds for momentous long-term changes were being sown. In 1950 a young winemaker called Max Schubert was sent by Penfolds to study sherry making (Penfolds' core business) in Jerez, Spain; this was the first time a non-family member had travelled overseas. It so happens that he was able to detour by Bordeaux on the way home, where he was taken under the wing of one of the doyens of the Bordeaux wine industry, Christian Cruse.

Schubert was shown wines which he recalled were 'between 40 and 50 years old and which were still sound, and possessed magnificent bouquet and flavour'. It is a fair bet that at least some came from the twin vintages of 1899 and 1900, the best since phylloxera started to invade Bordeaux in the 1920s. He returned home determined to produce 'an Australian red wine that would last at least 20 years and be comparable with those produced in Bordeaux'. Grange was born, and it survived near strangulation in its early years by the vicious attacks of most of the wine cognoscenti, who simply didn't understand the wine.

In 1951 David Wynn went against the recommendation of the experts he had employed to evaluate the property, and purchased Chateau Comaum, now known as Wynns Coonawarra Estate. His father Samuel, founder of the Wynn family wine business, sent a brief but poignant telegram, 'Admiring your courage'.

In 1953 Gramps Orlando beat Yalumba in the race to obtain the first import licence for stainless steel pressure fermentation tanks from Germany, laying the ground for a radical change in making riesling and equally momentous changes in the style of the wine, ultimately moving to that of today.

From the late 1940s and through to 1962, Colin Preece was making superb red wines at Seppelt Great Western, in some instances single vineyard, single variety (hermitage), wines, but more frequently using wines from two or three vintages, with a core of one vintage (in the manner of non-vintage champagne), utilising different regions and different varieties.

In the Hunter Valley, Maurice O'Shea's exceptional palate produced hermitage-based reds* (some with a small percentage of pinot noir) from the 1920s right up to the time of his death, prior to the '56 vintage. I became familiar with these wines in the 1960s and '70s when,

---

* Until well into the 1980s, shiraz was called hermitage in the Hunter Valley, at Great Western in Victoria and in Coonawarra, but everywhere else it was known as shiraz. As a result of later EU wine accords, the adoption of shiraz became compulsory.

although difficult to find, they weren't prohibitively expensive.

But this was still an unsophisticated market. To coincide with the 1956 Melbourne Olympics, Orlando released its Barossa Pearl in a distinctive bulbous bottle. Guenter Prass, Orlando's chief executive, recalled much later, 'This launch would have been, without a doubt, one of the most successful launches of any wine style in the last 50 years in Australia. The wine instantly captured the imagination of the Australian public. For many years the supply of Barossa Pearl was rationed, and after bottling the five millionth bottle, the company stopped counting.'

It was possibly just as well, for Hamilton's Ewell Moselle, and then Lindemans Ben Ean Moselle, were also to claim large slices of the market share. (It is a partial explanation, indeed, of the grotesque price of the German Blue Nun Liebfraumilch. To put that price into perspective, O.R. Crittenden, of Melbourne wine store fame, was offering the '54 Grange at 16/6 (retail) and the '55 Blue Nun Liebfraumilch for 31/6 in its November 1959 price list. Even generic Beaujolais – from '55, and doubtless very tired – was bringing 23/9 a bottle.)

July 1955 marked the first-ever domestic wine promotion campaign by the Australian Wine Board. It required an amendment to the Federal legislation: up to that time, the Board was only permitted to promote exports, although it was entirely funded by the wine industry via a levy on each tonne of grapes crushed. Plus ça change, indeed.

The campaign was successful, lifting sales of table wine over the next four years by 50 per cent, albeit from a miniscule base. Half the table wine market was dry red, the remainder split more or less equally between sweet and dry white wine, albeit with an elastic definition of what constituted dry wine. But it was not until 1966 that the total annual sales figure exceeded that of 1952.

In the midst of all this, the dead hand of the breweries was at work. In New South Wales they refused to handle flagons until the mid 1960s, and even then only of fortified wine. It was not until 1968/69 that they agreed to allow the sale of table wine in flagons.

Part of the tumult of the wine industry at the time passed me by, part did not. One Easter I led a group of friends down to Jindabyne on the Snowy River, well before the advent of Lake Jindabyne, and we camped at the nearby Moonbah River. A lovely, slow-flowing stream, it was then still full of only moderately educated trout. The only problem was that on this particular Easter it snowed more or less continuously between Canberra and Jindabyne.

Against the odds, I returned with a 1.5 kilogram brown trout, which was cooked and eaten with many preparatory beers and then a major assault (because it was so cold) on the Fiorelli plastic flagons of red wine we had providently purchased from Fiorelli direct – it most definitely stood outside the purview of the old boys running the Wine and Brandy Producers Association.

A male brown trout about to be returned to the stream, Mohaka River, Poronui Ranch, N.Z. (Note: not the unfortunate brown trout referred to in the text.)

A Life in Wine

Two memories endure from that Easter. One was the pyrotechnic effects of a nearly but not quite empty plastic flagon (closed) thrown onto the fire. The other was a drenched and near frozen friend lurching back to the fire announcing, 'I went down to the river to have a quiet pee, and it came up and hit me in the face.' In view of the absence of wind, and the head-to-toe saturation, we concluded that 'it' was indeed the river.

CHAPTER 3

1962:
A SHORT INTERMISSION

Notwithstanding my best efforts to the contrary, and a belated reali-sation that perhaps I wanted to be an architect after all (like my sis-ter Janet), I graduated on schedule with a BA LLB. The six years I spent at St Paul's College were the happiest, most carefree of my life, notwithstanding the location of the Law Faculty (in Phillip Street, Sydney, and not on the university campus as it is today) and the even greater distraction of three years as an articled clerk at Clayton Utz coinciding with the last three years of law study.

When, in early 1962, I completed my articles (to Sir Hector Clayton, a wonderful, larger-than-life man) and announced my

OPPOSITE: *A portent of things to come: the framework of the Coldstream winery is erected.*

intention to go overseas for the remainder of the year, I was told by the firm that there would be no job for me when I returned. Without expressly saying so, I thought this was the best news I had heard in ages, and it removed any lingering obstacle to my trip.

I went with long-term school and St Paul's College friend Jack Friday (we had shared a room as freshers at St Paul's, bonded by the fresher-bashing which was then very much part of the culture). We sailed on the Lloyd Triestino *Fairsea*, and came face to face with the first non-Australian beer (Oranjeboom) and wine (Bolla Soave) of our lives. By the time we reached England we were experts in a range of new alcoholic and culinary areas.

In fairness to my parents, I must add that as a result of continued trips after the Second World War, they had considerable knowledge of French and Italian food, then a rarity in Australia. It would be gilding the lily to suggest that my mother was a pioneer of fusion cuisine, but she was a very good cook – one of my favourite dishes was her blanquette de veau. When my sister married her husband Gordon in 1955, the wedding reception was held at our house, and the food was orchestrated by Johnny Battista, former chef at the Italian consulate and by then running one of Sydney's first up-market Italian restaurants, the Grotto Capri in Kings Cross. He served (amongst other things) ravioli and cassata, both novelties for most of the attendees (though not my sister, who had made the same journey as I would in 1961 when she finished her architecture degree, and had lived and worked in Italy for some time).

Some of this had rubbed off on me. I had begun to cook, and my dreams centred on obtaining a Christmas job washing dishes at the Stuttgarter Hof, an Austrian restaurant in Taylor Square. I was quite happy to go without pay, simply to see what went on in the kitchen. For one reason or another, I failed to put the proposition to the restaurant, taking the second-best option of eating there regularly. It seems strange now, but not then: there was a very active Chinatown, and more than a handful of Italian trattorias, particularly in the back suburbs of town and in Leichhardt, but no French restaurants to speak of, other than the Alouette. Melbourne had a far more diverse and sophisticated history of fine food than Sydney.

But I digress. Our plan on arrival in England was to obtain jobs as schoolteachers, and on somewhat spurious grounds we obtained cut-price accommodation at University House, supposedly run for students from overseas undertaking further studies in the United Kingdom. To our surprise, we were unsuccessful in our application for teaching jobs – apparently something to do with our lack of experience – and we ended up working for F.S. Stowell, a subsidiary of Whitbread Brewery.

It was situated in a grimy section of the east end of London, and mainly underground. The buildings had been built by the East India Company, and partially retimbered with oak beams from ships taken during Nelson's defeat of the French Navy. There were two arms to the Stowell business: wine and spirits. All the products were bottled and packaged on the premises (although some of the labels didn't suggest that). On a metaphorical flip of the coin, Jack was assigned to the wine team, I to the spirits section.

The entire premises were bonded, and thus under customs supervision. Cars were routinely and thoroughly searched when they left, as were any bags carried by those leaving on foot. Down in the bowels of the buildings were the bottling halls, each with a glassed-in island in which a customs man worked, and (theoretically) watched what was happening on the workplace floor.

We were each issued with a brown dustcoat, and for an officially obscure reason, a small duralex glass which I came to realise held the equivalent of three nips (or standard drinks) of spirits (or wine). Given that we had the choice of beer, tea or coffee at morning tea, lunch and afternoon tea, it was not immediately apparent to me what the function of the glass might be.

I didn't have to wait long. As we clocked on for the shift, and the ancient, pressure-activated bottling line came to life, most of my fellow workers would walk up to a filler head, push its rubber rings upwards, and fill his glass. The contents were drunk in one big gulp, and the process repeated two or three times. Those who abstained did so because they preferred some other form of spirits to that being bottled at the time.

It was a classic portfolio: gin (the least favoured), cognac, scotch whisky, and two rums, the fine old dark (at 44/9) outselling the pale (41/9) by a ratio of five to one. The only difference between the two was the caramel colouring we added to the fine old dark. So if it were gin on the line, those wanting something else would scuttle off at the first opportunity down another floor to rooms honeycombed with hundreds of pigeon holes for labels – and the squirrelled-away bottles of favourite tipple.

Bond warehouses and bottling facilities work with a margin of tolerance. What comes in under bond must equal that which leaves (without duty calculated at the time of departure) but with a bottling tolerance or wastage of 5 per cent. Since by far the greatest amount of cost to F.S. Stowell lay in the duty it had to pay, and since in those days precise quantities were impossible to measure (for example, we had to break-back overproof scotch and rum with water, and container sizes varied), Stowell was happy enough as long as it didn't have to pay duty on non-existent stock – in other words, if the 5 per cent was not exceeded.

For its part, the Customs Department was vigilant in ensuring that no bottles left the premises in the care of the workers. But it turned a Nelsonian eye to consumption on the premises provided you turned your back to the glass cage when having a drink, or made sure a bottle being taken downstairs was concealed in your dustcoat.

Not only were the halls very ancient, but the floors were very dirty. They were apparently thoroughly cleaned once a year, during the Christmas close-down; other than that, cotton waste was swept across them after work each Friday. The surface was an unappetising compound of machine oil, remnants of cigarette butts and spit.

After I had been working there for several weeks, we were scheduled to bottle rum for the first two days of the week, and the over-proof rum was pumped into a vertical, enamelled, closed vat. Then, unexpectedly, we were told to bottle gin for the next five days. Under some customs by-law, the vat of rum was sealed, except for a glass tube down its side to show the level of the fluid inside. The tube just happened to have a small tap at its bottom end, and this was not sealed.

So for most of the five on the spirits line, the tap provided the fuel to get through the week of the despised gin. The chickens came home to roost halfway through the following week. When the rum had been broken down, caramelised and bottled, there was a serious deficiency, on which the company nonetheless had to pay duty. The deficiency was well over a bottle per person per day; my own contribution was minor, my fellow workers being serial alcoholics.

Head office came the following morning; a repeat of this kind would result in instant dismissal for us all. Duly chastened, we turned our attention to the next bottling task, which was Ballantyne's

---

FOLLOWING PAGES: *The view from the front verandah of the author's house, Yarra Yering winery in the foreground.*

Scotch Whisky. The side flaps on the label claimed that the scotch was 'Blended and Bottled in Scotland', which caused no concern to those of us who knew this wasn't always true.

The scotch, too, had to be broken back, and passed through an open trough with a floating ball valve exactly like a toilet cistern, which prevented the trough from over-filling. Except for this day, when it malfunctioned, allowing a significant amount of scotch to flow onto the floor unnoticed. There was no discussion: we simply got to with brooms, scrapers, dustpans and whatever else would collect the scotch and put it back into the trough. The next several hundred bottles were an unusually dark colour, but the evidence was concealed in sealed cardboard cartons, and the feared repercussions did not eventuate. While there was no health issue involved – alcohol at this level is a great antiseptic – I fancied the taste may have been as unusual as the colour, but I decided against making myself a consumer taste test pig.

After six weeks of this, working every day, going out every night and embarking on excursions each weekend, Jack and I decided we simply had to have a night at our lodgings to do some urgent washing and ironing (we had been using the Social Lion's fallow rotation system), and write some long-overdue postcards. Jack's father was head of Dewars Whisky in Australia – it was through his contacts that we got the job at Stowells – so we had a hitherto untapped supply of Dewars in our rooms.

I arose the following morning feeling fine and full of virtue, until I noticed the empty bottle of Dewars. After some discussion, it was agreed that I had consumed two-thirds, Jack (at best) the remainder. I instantly understood how quickly one could start down the road to alcoholism, and equally quickly said, 'That's it, we are out of here.'

And so we filled our Ford Thames delivery van with camping gear, food and our other possessions and headed off to France. Over the next three months we traversed Europe, from the south of Spain to the heel of Italy, France, Switzerland, Austria, Germany and finally Scandinavia. We camped everywhere (in camping grounds) with our two-man tent; cooked for ourselves; and purchased whatever wine was local and cheap. Two discoveries were just how amazingly cheap Spanish brandy and wines were, and (on our first night on the outskirts of Rome) that the round wicker-basket Chiantis we had consumed the previous night came in 1.5 litre configurations, as well as the 750ml bottles we thought we had drunk. The vinous Magic Pudding gave us both monumental hangovers. This was artisanal chianti at its most lethal level; even my Fiorelli training was no protection.

Looking back, I have no recollection of paying any attention to the location of Bordeaux, Burgundy, Beaujolais, the Rhône, Alsace and so forth. In wine terms they were still beyond my horizons, and if we passed through, it was only as part of moving from one end of France to another.

On the other hand, there was a never-to-be-forgotten night in the Hofbrauhaus in Munich with two Australian girls we had met at the camping ground. Then there was the night in Vienna when we once again had company crouched in the back of the van, discovered by police doing a vehicle insurance check. Our green insurance papers were for two people only (there were, after all, only two seats), so four were evicted on the spot.

We then played cat and mouse with increasingly agitated police until we agreed with each other that we would all meet at the front of the Opera House. We didn't have the faintest idea where we were when finally, irrevocably, forced to separate, but reckoned we would all find our way to such a landmark – which, scruffily dressed, we duly did just as the dinner suits and evening gowns of the opera patrons were emerging at the end of the performance.

As autumn arrived, Jack returned to England to meet his parents, and I went on alone through Denmark and Norway. As I went further north, the days shortened, but the intensity of the silence of the Norwegian fjords was mesmeric, the scenery ever more grand. Camping grounds were no more, so I slept in the back of the van on top of my assorted possessions. When, finally, thick ice started to form on the inside of the van's roof each night, I reluctantly turned south.

I returned home by plane, travelling via the United States, starting in New York, then Boston, Mississippi and San Francisco, courtesy of medical and life insurance friends of my parents (my father was, amongst other positions, chief medical officer of the AMP Society). I arrived in San Francisco at the height of the Cuban crisis, to see troops guarding the Golden Gate Bridge and the daily news leaving no doubt that the world was on the brink of war. I was strangely fatalistic about the possibility of being stranded in California, but once again wine played no part in my life. Spirits (and my training at Stowells) were the order of the day; the Napa Valley was never discussed.

OPPOSITE: *Author's children Angus (left) aged five and Caroline (right) aged seven, hard at work foot-stamping a micro ferment of pinot noir at Brokenwood.*

47

CHAPTER 4

1963–68: THE ACCUMULATION

Despite the warnings before I left, I found there was a job for me at Clayton Utz after all, and before long I had set up house in Neutral Bay with Michael Hornibrook (six years later to be my best man at my wedding) and others, all from the same law firm.

The year before, Len Evans had become the first regular wine columnist with his 'Cellarmaster Says' column in the *Bulletin* magazine, drawing upon his position as Food and Beverage manager (in charge of 350 staff, including 50 cooks and apprentices) at Australia's first international hotel, the Chevron in Kings Cross.

In my latter days at university I had been a client of the hotel, arriving with college friends to descend on something never before seen in Australia: a fixed-price, self-serve, smorgasbord lunch which

---

OPPOSITE: *In a corner of the Turramurra cellar.*

allowed you to eat as much as you possibly could. In our case, that was an indecent amount.

In Melbourne, Walter James was producing his beautifully written books-cum-monographs on wine, and Frank Doherty was an occasional columnist. In Sydney, Frank Margan began contributing a weekly wine choice for the *Sunday Telegraph*, a few words on the bottom of one page of a thick newspaper consigned to the bin once I had devoured his words.

Despite the success of the promotional campaign from 1956 to 1959, domestic sales of Australian wine were still below the levels of 1951 and 1952, and both the 1962 and 1963 annual reports of the Australian Wine Board were fully of gloomy warnings about stagnant domestic and export markets and 'wine grapes surplus to winemakers' requirements'.

Beneath the surface, however, things were changing. As part of the upcoming move back from fortified to table wine, first Mildara and then Penfolds began buying and planting land in Coonawarra, as well as buying what wine they could from Redmans (which had bottled the first Rouge Homme wines in 1952, having previously sold all the wine in bulk).

In 1959 Glen McWilliam planted cabernet sauvignon at Hanwood, Griffith; he planted riesling and gewurztraminer the next year. The 1963 Hanwood Cabernet Sauvignon was a brilliant wine, still impressive 45 years later, but remained one of those freakish first vintages, in some ways similar to the 1963 Mildara Coonawarra Cabernet Sauvignon, nicknamed Peppermint Pattie. It was the first labelled Mildara Coonawarra wine, but not in fact the first crop from the vineyard. (Ironically, if a wine with such all-encompassing mint were to be made today it would be dismissed out of hand as a caricature.)

Lindemans became active in the Clare Valley, buying substantial quantities of wine from Stanley Leasingham, which was steadily increasing its estate vineyards. Indeed, it sought to acquire Stanley in the early 1960s, finally backing away and (in 1965) purchasing Rouge Homme.

The industry as a whole, however, was still rooted in the past. In its 1963 report the Australian Wine Board observed:

It is disappointing that clearances of fortified wines in Australia were the lowest for seven years ... The market for sweet fortified wines has remained fairly static for the past ten years. The Board believes there is a big potential in Australia for sweet wines but has not been able to do much to promote these products on a national basis ... There is no indication that the market in Australia for sweet (fortified) wines is likely to increase to any extent under the present circumstances.

However, it grudgingly admitted, 'On the other hand the trend in table wine is most satisfactory.'

On 1 January 1965 Len Evans became the first National Promotions Executive with the Australian Wine

Board. Our paths were still to cross, but he recounted that it was left up to him to write his own job description and responsibilities. Between 1964/65 and 1969/70 red wine sales rose by over 150 per cent; Evans developed a plan for the promotion of rosé, summarily rejected by the Board because (in its words) 'not everyone makes a rosé'. Within two and a half years he had effectively worked himself out of a job, moving on to found The Rothbury Estate and his one and only restaurant-cum-wine shop, Bulletin Place.

Equally important was the 1963 decision by Sydney-based Dr Max Lake to buy a hillside block of rich, red soil opposite McWilliam's Rosehill vineyard on Broke Road in the Hunter Valley. He flew in the face of convention by daring to suggest that a city dweller with no previous winemaking experience could plant a vineyard (with friends, including Len Evans), bring it to maturity, and then proceed to make wine – a few dozen bottles in 1965, the first significant vintage in 1966 (appropriately, twin vintages among the Hunter Valley's all-time best).

If this were not enough, he turned his back on shiraz, and planted the first cabernet sauvignon to be introduced to the Valley for 50 years or more. His inspiration was a 1930 Dalwood Cabernet Petit Verdot which he had tasted not long before starting Lake's Folly, as his winery was (and is) called.

These events were happening unknown to me, but I was part of the statistical fabric of the times. For the first time in my life, I began buying wines in quantities greater than my consumption, and I established my first cellar – underneath the double bed in my room at the Neutral Bay house.

We lived a free-wheeling bachelor existence, typified by a particular weekend jaunt to Pittwater and the hiring of an aluminium dinghy plus outboard to go fishing with our girlfriends. I had been an avid fisherman since I was seven, visiting all the wharves on the south side of Sydney harbour, and being inducted into fly fishing in the streams around Jindabyne on the Snowy Mountains by my father by the time I was 12. Trout fishing was a longtime passion of most of the members of my family.

On that sunny Pittwater day, I had a heavy line baited with a whole fish on a large hook left in the water 'just in case' while we fished with much lighter tackle for tailor and yellowtail. After several hours, we were about to move on when I realised the heavy line had started to move. Later again, I finally got the shark on the end to the side of the dinghy. No amount of entreaty by the girls was going to persuade me to cut it loose, and even though it was only slightly shorter than the dinghy, I was adamant that it was coming on board.

As I grasped its tail and proceeded to heave it into the boat, the only thing preventing the girls from jumping into the water was the thought that the shark's mate might be lurking there, seeking revenge. I grabbed an oar, held it vertically with its top pointed downwards, and brought it down with all my force towards the shark's head. It lunged at the critical moment, and I missed my mark, leaving a strange dent in the bottom of the dinghy.

Eventually the shark was subdued, but it was clear that the fishing (and a degree of friendship) was over. Ashore, I was equally reluctant to abandon my trophy, but how to get it home? Tom Lehrer wrote a song about hunting many years ago, and we basically followed the Lehrer lyrics:

> You sit there looking cute,
> and when something moves, you shoot.
> I tied them to my fender
> and got them home somehow –
> two game wardens, seven hunters,
> and a pure-bred Jersey cow.

The shark was stowed in the boot rather than on the fender, but was too long to be doubled up. By tying the boot lid onto the bumper bar, we had the middle section of the shark secure. Its head was poking out one side, its tail the other. It was Sunday afternoon, with heavy traffic heading back to Sydney, and it is fair to say the shark gained considerable attention on the trip home.

The third member of the house – who for obvious reasons shall go nameless – was leading an irregular life, partially due to an affair with a married lady in the days when photography was part and parcel of divorce proceedings. Michael and I knew he would be returning home later that evening with his friend and – in accordance with usual practice – would carefully barricade his door from the inside before turning on the light.

We artfully placed the shark in his bed on its back; its head rested on a pillow, and we arranged a bouquet of flowers in its large upturned mouth. It all went more or less according to plan, and the shrieks and oaths from the bedroom were appropriately loud.

With a measure of calm restored, the shark was evicted onto the overgrown front lawn. (When, some time later, the lawn was mown, we discovered an extra set of steps and various other features.) The shark settled out of sight and, for a few days, out of mind, until it started to emanate smells reminiscent of my brother's stingray.

The moment of reckoning came when a delivery of four dozen bottles of Lindemans 1962 Reserve Bin 2222 Riesling very nearly came to grief because the aroma caused the delivery man to lose control of his trolley. He departed with a volley of imprecations about 'that fish'.

A permanent disposal plan was needed. There was no way the shark was going to fit in our garbage bins, so Michael and I tossed to determine who should be responsible for its disposal. He lost, and disappeared with the shark. I assumed he would take it to the harbour – ashes to ashes, dust to dust – but he was back rather sooner than anticipated. 'What did you do with it?' I asked. 'I put it in a be-tidy bin in Forsyth Park' – this was a nearby sports field, where, I seem to remember, girls played volleyball.

Back at the office, our behaviour was more circumspect. I was working hard, intending to become a barrister, and with no thought of staying with the firm as a solicitor. There had, in fact, been no admissions of partners for almost ten years; this was a source of discontent for some, but not me. Then, out of the blue, an offer of partnership was made to Michael, John Stowe (also later to become a barrister) and myself. It was an easy decision for the other two, less so for me, but in the end I, too, accepted.

The immediate consequence was a large increase in my income, not (even in real money terms) anywhere close to the near-obscene levels of today, but substantial nonetheless. I moved into a new apartment in Paddington, and my wine cellar began to increase rapidly. First it filled the built-in floor-to-ceiling linen cupboards, a source of pride; the overflow was taken to my parents' cellar.

I soon found that my mother, assuming any bottle not of Lindemans origin was fair game for cooking, had decapitated some prize bottles. To head off further mistakes, I tore up a bed sheet and bedecked each of my bottles with a very obvious white bow around its neck.

Buying trips to the Hunter Valley increased, and I started to scour wine shops for treasures. Then in 1966/67 I went to wine education lessons conducted by Len Evans for the Wine and Brandy Producers Association, and introduced myself. In 1968 I planned a three-state, two-week wine odyssey – for Michael, John Gleeson (who in later years became a distinguished barrister) and myself – which swung through southern New South Wales via Mildura (where we purchased precious bottles of 1963 Mildara Coonawarra Cabernet Sauvignon and slightly less precious bottles of the Cabernet Shiraz of the same year) then through all the regions around Adelaide before heading back via Coonawarra through Victoria.

Our car was a V8 Valiant owned by John Gleeson's parents; while large by the standards of the time, it was soon dangerously overloaded, so we hired an Avis trailer in Adelaide, striking a passing friendship with several of the Avis counter girls. More memorable was the day we were driven around McLaren Vale and the Clarendon Hills region by the septuagenarian Ken Hardy (of Thomas Hardy) in his elderly, black Rover 90. Because two of us were in the back, and Ken Hardy was a gentleman of the old school (something inherited by Sir James Hardy), he considered it polite to look us in the eyes while discoursing.

When, as he twisted around to talk to those in the back seat, and his already tenuous grip on the steering became even more irrelevant, we knew for a fact that he had negotiated some deal with all the patron saints of travellers. Although it made concentration difficult for us as we sat rigid, waiting to shout a warning about the seemingly inevitable collision, his accounts of the family's involvement with McLaren Vale over the preceding 100 years were vastly entertaining.

One long-planned visit was to the Seaview Winery, still owned by Ben Chaffey and family. We had purchased as much as we could find of Seaview's 1961 Cabernet Sauvignon in Sydney over the preceding 12 months or so, and had noticed some real or imagined bottle variation that seemed to coincide with small but evident variations in the printing of the labels. John Gleeson, then a pugnacious barrister, was determined to get to the bottom of it all, and was given the task of cross-examining Ben Chaffey. When the moment came, he went to water, fawning and simpering.

The quaint purchase of some elderly half bottles of Henschke Rosé (found in a sack in a corner of the cellar); my meeting with Brother John Hanlon at Sevenhill in the Clare Valley, who was followed in 1972 by the twinkle-eyed, rosy-cheeked Brother John May; and being greeted by a youthful (well, it's true, so were we) Phil Laffer at Rouge Homme are parts of a mosaic of memories.

By the time we reached Rutherglen, our box trailer was as dangerously overloaded as the car, so when we purchased large quantities of Bailey's 1954 and 1958 Dry Red, they were consigned by rail to Darling Harbour goods yard, and collected with great pride and joy a week later. The '58 became our standard barbeque red, and the '54 was kept for slightly more formal occasions.

CHAPTER 5

IT GETS SERIOUS 1969–70

This was a period of great change, for the wine industry and my involvement in it, and for me personally.

I was certainly doing my bit to help sales along. By the time I was married, in April 1969, I had mini-cellars stretching from Sydney to Moss Vale – my parents had returned to live there after selling their house in Victoria Road. Liz (my first wife) and I built a house in Turramurra with an underground cellar carved out of solid Hawkesbury sandstone (under a split level house above). It was meant to be half the length of the house, but owing to an error by the builder (believe me, it was), the excavation ran the entire length of the house.

I had already learnt that Tooths Brewery was selling its old beer bottle crates, which were made of galvanised iron with wooden runners on the top sides (to act as handles), and had purchased several hundred. Now I was a serious buyer, hiring an Avis truck and buying

OPPOSITE: *Author playing the fool in the days of long sideburns.*

500 crates at a dollar each. I still have them as part of the racking system in my cellar in the Yarra Valley; standing seven high and back to back, they are self-supporting.

In those far-off days, I knew exactly where every bottle in the cellar was to be found, and which bottles showed signs of the corks failing – which resulted in immediate consumption of the offending bottles. Now corks are my arch-enemy, with several thousand bottles in my cellar (slowly retreating from its high of 15,000 bottles) desperately needing to be recorked (or thrown out). There never seem to be enough hours in the day, or days in the week, to adequately care for my cellar.

The acquisition of Rouge Homme by Lindemans in 1965 was the first of a series of rapidly escalating takeovers. In shorthand form they were (listing the acquirer first, the target second):

- 1966: Seager Evans UK/Glenloth Wines;
- 1969: Consortium/Hungerford Hill; Reed Consolidated UK/JY Tulloch; WR Carpenter/ Arrowfield;
- 1970: Reckitt & Colman UK/Gramps Orlando and Morris; Allied Vintners/Glenloth and Seaview; Nathan & Wyeth/Quelltaler; Reed Consolidated/ McLaren Vale Wines and Ryecroft; Hungerford Hill/ Chateau Reynella;
- 1971: HJ Heinz US/Stanley Leasingham; Phillip Morris US/Lindemans; Rothmans UK/Hungerford

A Life in Wine

Hill and Chateau Reynella; Dalgety Estates/
Krondorf;

- 1972: Allied Vintners/Wynns; Davis Consolidated/
Baileys; Dalgety Estates/Saltram, Stonyfell and
Loxton Estate;
- 1974: Hermitage Wines/Elliots Wines; Gilbeys UK/
Tulloch and Ryecroft; and
- 1975: Gollin & Co/Saxonvale; Tooths Brewery/
Penfolds.

Within the next ten years, every one of these
businesses had been on-sold by chastened acquirers who
had found that the wine industry was not the pot of gold
they had imagined it to be; and all but one of the foreign
ownerships had reverted to Australian hands.

At the end of the decade there were other signs, too,
that the industry was emerging from a long period of
stagnation. In 1970 plantings hit 60,000 hectares for the
first time, up from 56,000 hectares five years earlier. Total
grape production had risen even more convincingly, with
286,000 tonnes crushed versus 176,000 tonnes in 1965
(itself a record). Indeed, even though plantings were due
to decline significantly in the mid 1980s, production kept
on a more or less continuous upwards trend as the yield
per hectare increased. The most dramatic change was
brought about by the red wine boom: 1970 recorded sales
of 25 million litres compared with 9.6 million litres in
1965 (and surging to 36 million litres in 1975).

For the first time, too, there was a monthly publication providing tasting notes and recommendations. In April 1968 Len Evans published the first issue of *The Wine Buyer*. 'There is a need,' he wrote, 'to know what are the available good wines and blends, where they are, the best years of certain areas, the cellaring future of reds and whites, various winemaking characteristics and, above all, quality and value.'

He reviewed 11 wines, including 1967 Lindemans Hunter Riesling Bin 3255 at $1.55, pointing to the history of the preceding vintages back to 1959; Mildara Golden Bower Riesling (in fact, like the Lindemans wine, Hunter Semillon) at $1.05; and 1964 Penfolds Clare Riesling Bin 24FR, at $1.70, which he knew wasn't true riesling, and – amazingly – speculated might be gruner veltliner 'having seen these grapes in full bearing in Austria'. It was in fact crouchen, and not surprisingly, he said he preferred it when young.

The high point of the issue was a comparative review of 1962 Chateau Lafite ('The wine costs money – something over $9 a bottle – yet it cannot be called expensive') and 1962 Penfolds Grange Hermitage. Here he wrote, 'The '62 Grange is also fairly high-priced, yet is very much worth the money. At $2.40 it is extremely good value, though I dislike seeing some hotels charging as much as $4 in their bottle departments just because the wine is in short supply.'

I'm less sure he would still hold to his conclusion that 'the '62 Grange is the best Grange there has been; the '53 had marvellous oak balance, the '55 won all the gongs, but is now fading'. Offered the choice of the '53, '55 or '62 today, I know his choice would have been '53 first, '55 second and '62 third.

In his introduction to issue number 12, for July–August–September 1969, he wrote:

ABOVE: *Author left, John Rourke right – Virgins Choir singing in Bulletin Place for Len Evans' 40th birthday.*
FOLLOWING PAGES: *The Yarra Valley cellar as it is today.*

I do apologise for the delay, but I have been incredibly busy opening my new premises [at Bulletin Place] in Sydney. I hope this in future to be a centre for all wine lovers. Initially, we have opened the store in the cellar and plan to have the private luncheon club open soon.

I am delighted to offer to all *Wine Buyer* subscribers membership of this club, and an application form is enclosed. Membership is free, and attendance is non-obligatory, so interstate subscribers may join without feeling they have to fly

to Sydney for the occasion, I should be delighted to see them whenever they are in town.

The Wine Buyer shall continue ... The price remains the same for twelve issues [his underlining] whether this takes one year or two to complete ...

They were days of another era, pre-fax, and (emphatically) pre-email. Gentlemen and gentlewomen were not forced to rush the finer things of life. I'm not too sure the free membership of what became the Bulletin Place Beef Room was a necessary sales pitch, but it was to play the central role in taking me into the hitherto largely unknown world of great French and German wine.

The late 1960s and early 1970s were strange times in the comparative pricing of Australian and imported wines. There was a brief but sudden surge in the prices of Bordeaux reds between 1969 and 1972, before a precipitous crash in 1974. However, substantial stocks of older vintages were on offer in Australia uninfluenced by the sharp increase in replacement costs in Europe.

I have before me as I write the 1971 price list of B.H. MacLachlan Pty Ltd, the then owner of Walkerville Wines in Adelaide. 1968 Lake's Folly was $37.25 per case, while 1962 Chateau Palmer (one of its greatest vintages, considered equal to or better than the '61) was $44.65 per case. 1953 Faiveley Les Saint Georges (the closest thing to a Grand Cru in Nuits St Georges) was $56.27 a case, the

'59 (a great vintage) $46.29 and 1961 Musigny $64.35 a case.

These were wholesale prices (including import duties), but there was no problem if you put in an order of the size that I did. In April 1972 Len Evans Wines had on offer a huge range, including 1947 Chateau Rouget (of Pomerol, and a great wine) at $19.25 by the bottle, or $186 by the case. 1966 Chateau Pichon Longueville was $6.75, 1966 Chateau d'Yquem $14.25 and 1966 Bienvenues Batard Montrachet $7.30 a bottle, or $66 a case.

Obviously enough, these and innumerable other wines were very tempting, but by this time I was both importing wines direct from Bordeaux and had commenced buying at Christie's Auctions in London. The Australian dollar was strong, at over 6 French francs, and there were no sales taxes on wines. In November 1970 I landed 52 dozen cases of wines, chiefly from St Emilion and Pomerol from the '62, '64, '66 and '67 vintages. The average FOB cost (FOB means free on board: freight and delivery costs included) was $26.95 a case! 1962 Cheval Blanc was by far the most expensive, at $114 per case; 1962 Chateau Nenin was $28.70 a case; 1967 Chateau L'Evangile $42.95. Across the Gironde river, 1966 Chateau Montrose was $25.45 and 1962 Chateau Lagrange $19.34 per case.

I'll stop this torture shortly, for it pains me as much as it does you, but in Len Evans's price list of February 1972 he had 1908 Chateau Montrose at $22.95 (a bottle), 1928 Chateau Gruaud-Larose at $36.90 (the most expensive of 40 or more old wines), 1949 Chateau Rouget at $8.50, 1937 Clos Vougeot (he didn't burden people with the names of the Burgundy producers) at $18, 1959 Richebourg at $15, 1959 Bonnes Mares at $11.10, and the great Domaine de la Romanée-Conti 1962 La Tache at $23 (he had acquired this from importer Emerald Wines some years previously at a fraction of that price).

The curiosity in the comparison between French and Australian prices I mentioned earlier came with Lindemans 1967 Hunter River Burgundy at $3.75 and 1962 Wynns Coonawarra Hermitage at $4. You could have a 1969 Beaune Les Greves for $4.65, a 1966 Chateau Rouget for $4.35, and a 1964 Chateau Climens for $4.30.

I said I would stop, and so I shall – even though within three years the price of French wines had fallen further in Europe (something I come back to later).

OPPOSITE: *The Brokenwood winery as it was in 1975, the rainbow a harbinger of many happy years to come.*

A Life in Wine

CHAPTER 6

BROKENWOOD 1970–83

It did not take the wisdom of hindsight to realise that just as Tony Albert, John Beeston and I (all habitués of Evans's Bulletin Place) were becoming deeply interested and financially involved with French and German wine, we also headed off to the Hunter Valley to search for land on which to plant a vineyard and erect a winery.

My reason for the plan was simple. Big city corporate law practice could easily suffocate all life and activity outside the law office. Even if you played sport or sailed a yacht, there had to be an element of compulsion – such as weekly involvement in a competition with others – that depended on your participation. Otherwise you would yield to a hangover, work in the office on a major transaction, watch school sport unless it was raining or find some other reason to leave your yacht moored, your tennis or golf postponed. A vineyard and winery provided the ultimate compulsion.

OPPOSITE: *Planting Brokenwood, 1971 – the worst job of all.*

We were initially interested in a 100-acre (40-hectare) block that still had signs of a long defunct vineyard on it, dating from around the turn of the 19th century. The asking price was $96 an acre, and while it was far larger than we needed, the price seemed fair. In 1969 there were only 591 hectares of vines planted in the Valley, not much up on the nadir of 468 hectares in 1956. By 1976 the boom had reached its height, and plantings soared to 4137 hectares. We were in on the ground floor.

Full of naïveté, we asked the NSW Department of Agriculture for a brief report on the suitability of the land for grapegrowing. The reply was basically negative; the soils were too heavy, with an acidic subsoil. We hurriedly backed off the purchase, little realising that the majority of the soils in the Pokolbin region fell into much the same category. (The block in question was subsequently purchased by The Rothbury Estate for a significantly higher price per hectare.)

Over 12 months later, a legal friend spotted a small notice in the NSW Government Gazette advertising the fact that a 10-acre (4-hectare) parcel of land in McDonalds Road, Pokolbin, was to be auctioned, with Crown Land terms of sale – 10 per cent of the capital to be paid on signing the contract, with 10 per cent each year thereafter plus interest at 4 per cent per annum.

Curiously, so it seemed, the auction was to be held mid-week, but this in no way deterred us. Indeed, off we went thinking we might be the only bidder. Unfortunately, Hungerford Hill, which already owned all the surrounding land, had the same idea, and had (I think unofficially) obtained the consent of the Cessnock Council for the erection of its planned winery on the site.

It is hard to say who got the biggest shock: we had gone expecting to pay somewhere between $200 and $500 (maximum) per acre

*Trying to work out a way of getting back to operating the water gun,
Brokenwood 1971.*

($500 to $1250 per hectare) and Hungerford Hill's expectation
must have been similar. Auction fever took hold, and we emerged
as the successful bidders at $1000 an acre ($2500 per hectare), an
outrageous and unprecedented price.

It was about as poor a block (from a soil/viticultural viewpoint)
as existed in the Hunter Valley, and the locals were unsure whether
we intended to establish a petrol station or a motel. What was clear
was that no one in their right mind could have possibly acquired
the block with the intention of planting a vineyard on any of it. But
of course it meant each of us only had to pay $333, plus interest at
4 per cent, each year; even in those days, this was an insignificant
sum. Hungerford Hill approached us in the weeks following the
auction, offering us a tidy little profit, but there was no way we were
going to take that bait.

A car-bonnet lunch with Tony Albert, Murray Tyrrell, John Beeston, Brokenwood 1971.

When we purchased the land it was timbered with innumerable scraggly spotted gums interspersed with a few ironbarks. The soil (or rather clay) was too heavy to support anything more. Yet it had seen better days.

Around the turn of the century, Dan Tyrrell gave a block of some 40 acres to the Cessnock Council for use as a sportsground and for public purposes; part around the perimeter was dedicated as a cemetery. A cricket ground was established in the middle 10-acre block.

The town was only 5 miles (8km) away, and in a few short years would undoubtedly spread over that distance. But the boom burst, Cessnock shrank, the cemetery was never used, and the cricket ground went to rack and ruin. When we purchased that 10-acre middle block in October 1970, the only reminder of its former glory was its Council zoning of 'recreation – open space'.

So through the summer months of 1971 the land was cleared and named; after toying with the idea of naming the vineyard Phylloxera Hollow, we settled for Brokenwood, a play on the Brokenback Range directly behind us, and the removed trees. The fallen timber was pushed into rows; some marvellous pyromaniac weekends were had as the windrows were burnt (with fire captain Murray Tyrrell having some nasty conflicts of interest); and then the increasingly boring and seemingly never-ending stick-picking commenced. No sooner did we make some impression on the bits and pieces of timber than the land would be worked again; like Jason's dragons' teeth, more sticks (tree roots and fractured branches) than ever would make their appearance.

By July, when the time for planting had arrived, the first 2 acres were still months away from being ready. The clay remained in great orange lumps, there were dips and hollows where tree stumps had been recently removed, and mounds where others remained. We had no business to be planting, but nothing could have stopped us. Up came the rootlings, propagated at the nurseries of Peter Smith at Mildura – 900 for 1 acre of Hermitage and another 450 for half an acre of Cabernet.

Time, it is said, brings perspective, heals all ... and does a great deal else. Forty years have done nothing to dim the agony I felt at the end of the first day's planting. Medieval torturers would have relished the opportunity of placing their victims in a Tyrrell planting team.

A tractor pulled a water cart at a slow, but unceasing, walking pace. Off the back ran two home-made water guns. These were hollow steel tubes with a crossbar at the top equipped with a hand-brake-like device; near the base a footrest protruded from one side, and 12 inches (30cm) below was a toothed drill-bit about 3 inches

(7–8cm) in diameter. The operator plunged the gun into the ground by simultaneously leaping on the base footrest and pushing down on the crossbar with all his might, maintaining a twisting action at the same time. The handbrake was pressed to release water to fill the hole.

This all took two seconds. Two more paces and you drilled another hole. In well-cultivated sandy soil it would be an afternoon stroll. In uncultivated clay it was not. After 10 minutes on this infernal machine you rapidly retreated to one of the easy jobs – putting the rootlings into the recently excavated holes – surprised at the number of seemingly willing volunteers for the gun. Never mind; self-preservation was paramount.

So every 10 seconds you stooped to ground level (there was no time to kneel) and forcibly thrust the vine into the ground just as the gun was removed. The gun had a wicked knife-edge rim around the drill bit; after two vines, the rootlings were receiving a handy nutritional supplement of blood and bone.

Surreptitiously covering your wounds with mud, you thankfully changed places with the third member of the team, who was looking decidedly pale around the gills and wasn't breathing too well. Had he seen the terrible wounds you had suffered and couldn't stand the sight of blood? Never mind; self-preservation was paramount.

Clasping aching back with maimed hand, you stood erect, breathing crisp country air, and took on the task of stamping the earth around the recently inserted vine. With horrible finality it dawned on you that this was the worst job of all. It involved an especially excruciating form of running on the spot – liquid streams of fire coursed up and down aching shins, and the tractor and water-cart were moving inexorably away from you. How to get back onto the gun became an obsession ...

A Life in Wine

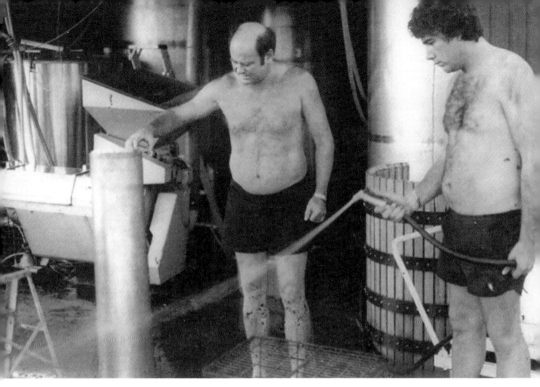

ABOVE: *Winemaking is a dirty job, Brokenwood, late 1970s.*
BELOW: *Cleaning picking crates, Brokenwood circa 1973. Author at centre back.*

Miraculously, the vines grew and grew well. Any 'strike' in excess of 90 per cent (nine out of ten vines surviving) is good; ours was around 95 per cent. Right through that growing season the vines flourished, and even in late May 1972, when the rest of the district was its customary drab brown, the Brokenwood vines were stridently green.

A year passed; winter came. Hurriedly we decided to build what was euphemistically called a tractor shed and to install a 91,000 litre underground water tank. The tractor shed was to have a kitchen, shower and toilet; and although the Council health department might not have approved, we intended to make our first vintage there. In fact, the shed was ultimately completed around Easter, some three months after vintage. In the meantime, our winemaking equipment – crusher, hand-operated press and open stainless steel fermentation tank – had been delivered to Rothbury.

John Beeston had spent hours on the telephone to obscure Italian machine-makers in Victoria who evidently understood the needs of small-scale peasant farmers in their homeland, and saw nothing extraordinary in the commissions they received for the tiny crusher and press. John's father-in-law had lovingly supervised the making of a 1360-litre stainless steel fermentation tank, so we were equipped.

With no small degree of tolerant amusement we were allowed to set up our machinery in a corner of the then largely empty bottle storage area of Rothbury. The chief winemaker was Gerry Sissingh, whom I had met at Lindemans all those years before. It was he who gruffly told us to press the incompletely fermented hermitage, and allow the fermentation to finish in barrel when we announced that we had to go back to Sydney for our law firms. 'I'm not going to look after an open fermenter for you. The wine will be far safer in barrel,' thundered Sissingh. Little did we know that we were emulating the technique used by Max Schubert for Grange.

That year we made three hogsheads of hermitage and one of cabernet. Fifteen dozen Hermitage and 15 dozen Cabernet were bottled straight; the balance went into a blend of 84 per cent hermitage and 16 per cent cabernet. Seventy-five dozen of the blend were sold.

The 1974 vintage saw the shed erected; we stayed at the Hunter Valley Motel and commuted at all times of day and night to plunge fermenting vats, press must (the grape skins) and so on. John Beeston distinguished himself by diving headlong into the fermentation tank in a heroic but quite unintended endeavour to recover an errant thermometer. Twenty dozen Cabernet and 175 dozen Hermitage Cabernet were made and sold.

By January 1975 a graceful full-scale winery designed by architect friend John Rourke was – more or less – completed. Grape yields were up and fermenting juices ran blood-red, with an enormous depth of colour. Then came 1976, with yields no greater than 1975 – and this in a vineyard of maturing vines, planting having continued each year to 1974.

By 1977 the grim truth had dawned on us. The continued winter drought, allied with the poor clay country, had stopped the vines in their tracks. From a 4-hectare vineyard now fully planted with vines between three and six years old, we were able to produce for sale 185 dozen bottles of wine. It was quite obvious that we could not go on this way. We had a winery capable of handling 3000 dozen bottles of wine with ease, a bank overdraft of monumental proportions, and a seemingly insatiable market for our (non-existent) wines. Even though they were rationed, they sold out within weeks of being offered for sale.

ABOVE: *Brokenwood circa 1976, daughter Caroline, aged six.*
BELOW: *Beautifying some second-hand puncheons and rejecting the option of a hair comb-over.*

ABOVE: *The bottling team – how to change one mindless job for another. Author at centre.*

BELOW: *My Range Rover, circa 1977, with five-year-old son Angus.*

Our show results may well have had something to do with that: we first exhibited at the Hunter Valley Show in 1976 and won the trophy and the only silver medal in the small maker red class with our '75 vintage reds; we repeated this in 1977 with our '76s; then at the Sydney Show in 1978 (the first year the size of the class was sufficiently reduced to allow very small vineyards to enter) we topped the small maker class with 18 points, just missing out on a gold medal.

By sheer coincidence, Hungerford Hill decided to reduce the size of its vineyard, and one of the blocks on offer adjoined Brokenwood. We negotiated an option with Hungerford Hill, entitling us to pick the grapes from the 18-hectare block in the '78 vintage so we could be certain that (as we believed) the quality and style of the wine would be the same as that from the original Brokenwood block. We also bought in some grapes from Oakdale as a further comparison.

The wine from the Hungerford Hill block – known as the Graveyard – was identical to that from the original block, so we had no qualms about exercising the option. The '78 vintage was the third one badly affected by drought, and we experimented with a Coonawarra blend with one of the wines. Both this and the standard Hunter blend were to receive praise from numerous critics, and sold well.

The Coonawarra experiment was prompted in part by a unique and great Mildara Yellow Label '58 Hunter Coonawarra Cabernet Shiraz and in part by the fact that Brokenwood wines seemed to have far more in common with the wines of Coonawarra than most other Hunters did. They were deeper in colour, showed more wood, and the practice of early picking led to higher acid and seemingly fresher fruit flavour.

Then, just when we needed it most, the winter drought finally broke and one of those rarest of Hunter commodities – a perfect vintage – came along. In 1979 we made over 2200 cases of fine wine, far better at three months of age than any previous year. With further help from 14 new, fully handsplit Nevers puncheons (the first imported into Australia, according to their maker, Philippe Demptos), the future looked good. A small amount of the blend made its way to England, and received enthusiastic reviews from the foremost critics of the time.

Over the years I realised that in many ways winter was the best season of all in the Hunter. Even in the depths of winter there were endless days of clear blue sky and no wind. Bird calls had a special clarity, and colours were sharper and more pure. Frost under foot in the early dawn gave way to mornings warm enough to strip to shorts while working. Cane pruning is the hardest skill to learn in the whole canvas of grapegrowing and winemaking; after seven years I was finally at home among the tangled web of last year's growth and the shy buds which, come spring, would burst forth in wondrous profusion.

But the world had certain financial and logistical realities that required attention. Up to (and beyond) 1978 we had had to rely on a circle of close friends and supporters willing to give up weekends throughout the pruning season, Christmas holidays for bottling, and annual holidays during vintage. They worked long hours, particularly during vintage, there was no pay involved, and the sleeping

FOLLOWING PAGES: *The Rothbury Estate Purple Ribbon holders. The recipients of this highest honour, from left, the author (the first to receive the esteemed ribbon), John Beeston, Maggie Irwin, Ray Soper and Ian Irwin in the pinot noir block at Brokenwood, circa 1975.*

arrangements were strictly communal – double bunks in a single large upstairs loft. The logical move was to offer some of the most committed Brokenwood supporters among our friends a share. Six new partners, holding smaller interests, came in and formed the basis of a much larger – and, we hoped, viable – operation.

They were lured in part because they simply wanted to be part of it all, and partly by the lavish wine, food and socialising opportunities. Here, too, the locals had a field day, surmising that this was in fact a somewhat unusual house of ill fame. The rumour gained credence one morning during vintage when the girls decided to go topless while picking the shiraz on the Graveyard block. It wasn't long before a slow-moving procession of cars passed back and forth (with speedy U-turns once out of sight), the drivers all engrossed by the sights in the vineyard, accidents averted only because of the snails' pace at which the cars were proceeding.

The communal nature of the sleeping arrangements also gave rise to some moments which became part of the historical fabric of Brokenwood. One couple, feeling in need of some privacy one day, drove into the further part of the Graveyard block, got into the back seat of their car, and began to satisfy their mutual desire. She, looking upwards, suddenly stiffened, for their car was now surrounded by a group of fascinated young teenagers on horseback, courtesy of the local riding school. As you might imagine, disengaging without loss of decorum presented a major problem, and the riders were not to be easily distracted.

It was my turn to be embarrassed when, on one wet and muddy summer's day, Len Evans drove in in the British racing green Bentley Continental he then owned. For reasons I could neither then nor now adequately explain, dressed only in a mud-splattered pair of shorts and runners, I decided to give my best imitation of a crazed

A Life in Wine

ABOVE: *Len Evans's annual birthday parties required fancy dress –
here the theme was* The Great Gatsby.
BELOW: *Len Evans and Suzanne at front, the Bulletin Place front
row in formation at the back.*

ape, rushing towards the car scratching my armpits. Inside the car, Len Evans had just finished explaining to a visiting English Lord and wife that they were about to meet an interesting man who was both a partner in a distinguished Sydney law firm and a vigneron. Evans, being Evans, milked the moment for all it was worth, leaving me nowhere to hide, metaphorically or otherwise.

Another memorable event – by chance, also involving Len Evans and his Bentley – came on a Saturday in late January 1975, when a task force assembled at around 8am to pick our first pinot noir from the half-acre behind the winery. It was scheduled to last until late morning, and to be followed by a leisurely lunch. It was in fact all over by 9am, and the boot of the Continental held more or less the entire minuscule crop. As much in dismay as celebration we repaired to the winery to drink champagne until the planned early lunch, by which time John Beeston – a huge man, then with a considerable appetite for wine and food – had consumed a very large amount of one of his favourite drinks, champagne.

After lunch we agreed we would go yabbying in one of Murray Tyrrell's dams. When we came to the first barbed wire fence, John decided to do a backwards Fosbury flop, executed by simply backing up to the fence and leaning in the appropriate direction. The manoeuvre worked well in the sense that he finished up on the other side of the fence, but his back was not a pretty sight. As usual, I was the cook that night, so it was decided that I would go back to the winery with John, apply antiseptic cream to his numerous lacerations, and start preparations for dinner.

First aid completed, he fell into a deep, sonorous sleep in a lounge chair, waking just as dinner was being served. His (predetermined) contribution to the wine that evening was three bottles of 1916 Chateau Coutet to accompany the dessert. The meal went on until late, followed by a game of seven-card stud poker for some of us, and Beeston carried on as if it had been a perfectly normal day. Equally off-handedly, and seemingly none the worse for wear, his opening words at breakfast the next day were, 'Tell me, what was the Coutet like?', a tiny admission that his mental faculties may have been slightly impaired by the events of the previous day.

There were many more occasions, some even more hilarious but unrepeatable. Nonetheless, it became obvious by late 1982 that as well as expanding the partnership, we really had to hire a full-time winemaker. Brokenwood had the great good fortune to engage the services of Iain Riggs (from Hazelmere in McLaren Vale). He continues to guide the fortunes of Brokenwood to this day, as chief executive of what is a particularly successful winery – its Graveyard Shiraz is an acknowledged icon, and its semillons (and indeed all its wines) are in much demand both in Australia and in overseas markets.

My last vintage at Brokenwood was 1983, and it was a fiery send-off as temperatures soared. We arose to commence picking each morning at first light, finishing around midday. In anticipation of my move to Melbourne for Clayton Utz's embryonic practice in that city, I sold my share of Brokenwood to the other partners. Financial considerations driven by a divorce settlement certainly played a part, but there was also no way I could continue as an active partner, and anything less would not have satisfied me.

I have returned many times since with no sense of regret, just pride. Iain Riggs has transformed an economically fragile business into a robust and successful one. Young winemakers who gain vintage experience at Brokenwood treasure the time they spend there, and almost all have gone on to bigger and better things.

CHAPTER 7

BULLETIN PLACE 1969–83

While all this was happening, I and a like-minded group of friends had fallen under the spell of Len Evans and Bulletin Place. Before long, a group of four or five – always including John Beeston, Tony Albert and myself, who, in rugby parlance, formed the front row of Bulletin Place – had an unbreakable commitment to meet every Monday lunch to play the Options Game with Len Evans at the first table on the left as we came into the room. In its rudimentary form, it had been invented by Len (others have from time to time sought to take credit, but it was he who brought it forward), but with three pairs of legal eyes, and the crucible of practical experience, the rules were honed and refined over several years.

OPPOSITE: *Hermann Schneider (then of Two Faces Restaurant, Melbourne) presenting (L to R) John Beeston, author and Tony Albert with framed golden sovereigns. Inscription reads: 'If your wine (1975 Brokenwood) is as scarce as gold, you must be paid in gold.'*

The basic idea is that each person brings a bottle of wine; it is decanted into a bottle with a number or initials, but no other identification; and each person takes it in turn to ask questions about his wine (he alone knows the identity of it). Each question is in the form of a multiple-choice option; is this wine A, B or C?, and one of the options has to be correct.

We kept tally by means of 20c pieces: we all started with the same number, and had to throw a coin into the centre of the table each time we made a mistake. Since each person brought one bottle, the winner was the person with the most coins left. The pot of coins funded the purchase of lottery tickets, but they had a notable lack of success.

In the wild frontier days there was no limit on the number of questions asked. At that time, too, and later, we were accustomed to wines coming from the 19th century bobbing up. On one infamous occasion, Len Evans produced an intensely sweet, dark brown, olive-rimmed wine, the sweetness balanced by lingering acidity. 'Is this wine younger or older than 1870?' was his first question.

One after the other (each person took it in turn to answer a question first) we all opted for older. Wrong; in went the 20c pieces. 'Older or younger than 1880?' Older, of course. Wrong. More 20c pieces. By the time there was a mountain of coins, we learnt that the wine was from 1959. It was a celebrated Trockenbeerenauslese Kreuznacher Brüchs. (For the technically minded, it had lost its SO_2 protection early on, hence its colour, but the very high residual sugar – and acidity – protected it against oxidation as that term is commonly understood.)

As a result of that escapade, it was agreed that no more than two questions could be asked about vintage. Then there were questions that had nothing to do with the taste of the wine: was this

A Life in Wine

wine served to Bismark on such and such an occasion? These too were outlawed. Soon, too, you could not ask 'Is this wine from (say) Australia, or France or elsewhere?' We agreed that the last option could not itself contain limitless options. Next we decided that splitting vintages into non-consecutive groups was barred: you could ask 'Is this first from 1959 to 1961, second from 1962 to 1964 or third from 1965 to 1967?', but you could not ask 'Is this from 1959, 1962 or 1966 on the first hand, or 1960, 1961 or 1967 on the other?'

There were only two instances in which four options were allowed: the four great communes of Bordeaux (Haut Medoc, Graves, St Emilion and Pomerol) and the four communes of the Haut Medoc (St Estephe, Pauillac, St Julien and Margaux). The most obvious of all rule refinements came fairly early on in the piece: a limit of five questions per wine, with the tacit understanding that in a well-asked series, the last question would precisely identify the wine.

This wasn't entirely the end, however. The production of a Turkish Buzbag wine by Tony Albert, an Italian Picolit by John Beeston and a Fijian wine made from bananas (by me, to my shame) meant that all such wines were outlawed except on a pre-agreed 'Deviates Day', and even then there were two added requirements: first, the wine had to come from vitis vinifera grapes, and second, it had to be at the very least of agreeable quality. There was no way we were going to explore the gutters and back alleys of Eastern Europe or anywhere else.

On the other side of the coin, there were the special days, such as First Growth Bordeauxs; Grand Cru Burgundies; 1949 or earlier; even 1899 and earlier. We had jointly purchased many old French wines through Christie's auction house in London. Through the first half of the 1970s a number of factors coincided to make Australia a happy hunting ground for people such as us.

The Australian dollar was very strong against the pound sterling: at one point I purchased sterling for $1.29 – compared with over $2 for much of the 1990s. Moreover, the recession of 1974/75 had a disproportionately strong impact on the French wine industry, which was already reeling after a short-lived foray into the 1972 vintage by Japanese buyers (a dreadful year in Bordeaux, though unrecognised as great in Burgundy), followed by an even more precipitant withdrawal.

In 1975 you could buy the legendary '45 Mouton Rothschild for £280 a case at Christie's, the '49 for £210 a case, the glorious '49 Chateau Latour for £260 a case, and there was no duty to be paid on arrival in Australia.

The wines we purchased jointly with Len Evans were delivered to Bulletin Place, where they were sorted and distributed according to our respective entitlements. But in one shipment, a case of 1948 Domaine de la Romanée-Conti La Tache disappeared without trace or explanation. Enquiries and searches were made here, there and everywhere, but no '48 La Tache could be found.

Six months passed, and then an Evans's option wine turned out to be the 1948 La Tache. Pointed questions were asked, but Len was all innocence. 'I just found it in my rack,' he said. In those days wines from the Domaine de la Romanée-Conti were not uncommon, and it was clear that Evans was irritated by the fact that I zeroed in on the style before he had even asked the first question. But when another bottle of La Tache came forward and the last question was 'Is this the '47, '48 or '49?' my blood pressure soared. Of course I denied '48; and of course it was.

Over the course of the next year more bottles made their appearance, on each occasion causing increasing cries (and sobs) of outrage: surely it couldn't be, surely he wouldn't dare. The element of poker inherent in the options game suddenly took on a new dimension, but with Evans holding all the cards. Then finally the day came: the last twist of the knife, the last bottle of '48 La Tache. Evans, the very picture of virtuous innocence, announced 'Yes, I did find the case of La Tache, and I thought the best solution was to share the wine with you all.'

Time passed. The La Tache wounds slowly healed, and the risk of Evans's strangulation diminished. Then, one day, a wine with all the hallmarks of '48 La Tache was presented by Evans. With surgical precision, he operated on his patients, but as the last question was asked, he knew he had better speak quickly and convincingly if he were to avoid an attack on his life. 'I was walking down the street in London, and passed a wine shop. There, on display in the window, was a bottle of '48 La Tache. What could I do? I simply had to buy it.' It was a story he never tired of telling, and I never ascertained the truth or otherwise of his explanation.

Another Monday tradition was a seven-card stud poker game convened in Evans's office after the conclusion of lunch, augmented by friends who were not part of the lunch proceedings. The game continued until well into the night, occasionally until the early hours of the following morning. Over the years I was the most consistent winner, and I used my winnings to buy wine from Christie's. One particularly big win coincided with an auction at which a large number of mixed lots from the cellar of a Bordeaux wine merchant were offered. Each lot was of a string of vintages, the youngest 1938 (my birth year), the oldest stretching back in one or two instances to the 1870s.

I put in very low bids for all the lots with 1938 wines in them, and for a number of others which looked particularly interesting. I was not hopeful of much success, but to my utter surprise, I was the successful bidder for almost all the lots, and at levels well below my already modest bids. In the event, 50 dozen bottles with an average age of 60 years or so arrived in a specially built wooden crate.

In retrospect, I made one fatal error. I should have recorked all the bottles on arrival. I didn't, and my cellar was subsequently moved on several occasions, with periods of inaccessibility. While many bottles were consumed (I had, for example, long runs of vintages of Chateau Palmer and Chateau Pichon Lalande from 1904 to 1934 which gave rise to excellent dinners), many were lost due to cork failure. The fact that the landed, all-up cost of the wines was an average of $11 a bottle was indicative of the time, but was also the outcome of a series of well-timed strokes of luck.

It was against this background that the Single Bottle Club dinners took shape. They have been one of the strongest strands in my wine life. For some, they will seem almost obscenely over the top, in terms of both the rarity and the value of the wines consumed in such numbers at a single dinner. But for Len Evans, without whose inspiration and drive the dinners would never have come into existence, for myself and for the others in the Club, these events had a value which cannot be measured in monetary terms.

They were, and are, dinners which, by their very nature, cannot be repeated. Nor would we wish to do so even if it were possible: the world of great wine and great food still abounds with as yet unexplored possibilities.

The first dinner was held on 4 February 1977. It was not called a single bottle club dinner; it was simply a dinner given by Len Evans in honour of Michael Broadbent. But the essential ingredients were there: each person attending the dinner provided (well in advance) one or more bottles, or contributed to the overall cost.

A dinner in honour of Michael Broadbent, given by Len Evans at Bulletin Place, February 4, 1977

Menu

Old Wine Tasting

	Menu			Old Wine Tasting	
The Prime Minister; The Right Honourable Malcolm Fraser	Turtle Soup	Very Dry Oloroso	1795	Rudesheimer Apostelwein	1727
Michael Broadbent M.W.				Chateau Villemaurine	1898
Peter Fox	Sand Crab	Le Montrachet	1972		
James Halliday		(Domaine de la Romanée-Conti)		Chateau Ausone	1894
Ray Healey	Jahmoor Quails	Clos de la Roche	1921	Chateau Lafite	1893
Ray Kidd		(Barolet)			
Rudy Komon				Chateau Peyrabon	1878
Max Lake	Beef Medallions with Truffles	Chateau Haut Brion	1929		
Dan Murphy				Chateau Lafite	1874
Hermann Schneider	Raspberry Soufflé	Vouvray Liquoreux	1921		
Simon Seward		(Marc Brédif)		Sunbury Hermitage	1872
Murray Tyrrell		Chateau d'Yquem	1921		
				Chateau Gruaud Larose	1825
	Nuts and Muscatels	Quinta do Noval	1931		
Wine Attendants: John Parkinson and Anders Ousback		Seppeltsfield	1878	Chateau d'Yquem	1888

The menu for the dinner in honour of Michael Broadbent (then head of Christie's, London), led to the annual Single Bottle Club dinners.

Those attending apart from Evans and Broadbent were Prime Minister Malcolm Fraser, Peter Fox (who in the late '70s/early '80s provided the financial support Len Evans desperately needed and sadly later died in a car accident), Ray Healey (radiologist and accountant with a great wine cellar), Ray Kidd (managing director of Lindemans), Rudy Komon (leading Sydney art gallery owner), Max Lake (of Lake's Folly), Dan Murphy (the man himself), Hermann Schneider (owner of Two Faces), Simon Seward (Melbourne retailer and wholesaler of fine wine), John Parkinson (long-time friend and executive of Cellarmasters, since retired), Murray Tyrrell and myself. The wine stewards were John Parkinson and Anders Ousback, more of whom in a moment.

On this occasion (and only this one) the dinner was divided into two parts: a wine for drinking with each course, and 'An Old Wine Tasting' staged between the main course and the dessert. The dinner wines were 1795 Very Dry Oloroso, with Turtle Soup; 1972 Le Montrachet of the Domaine de la Romanée-Conti (DRC for short), with Sand Crab; 1921 Clos de la Roche (Barolet), with Tahmoor Quail; Beef Medallions with Truffles accompanied by 1929 Chateau Haut Brion; Raspberry Soufflé with 1921 Chateau d'Yquem and 1921 Vouvray Liquoreux of Marc Bredif (which held its own against the exalted d'Yquem); and coffee, nuts and muscadelles with 1931 Quinta do Noval (a legendary vintage) and 1878 Seppelt Para Liqueur, which had not then been officially released, as it was not 100 years old, only 99.

The Old Wine Tasting included a 1727 Rudesheimer Apostlewein, it having been agreed that this ancient riesling would be served as an aperitif in specially commissioned hand-blown glasses. Although the Prime Minister shared a genuine interest in wine and trout fishing (the latter with Len and myself), and although he was to participate (in one way or another) in a number of the early dinners, it is fair to say he was hard going, especially on this first occasion.

The dinners were always black tie (Evans would not dream of anything less) and we were standing, rather awkwardly engaged in desultory conversation, while more or less behind us, Anders Ousbach was opening the 1727 Rudesheimer. The incredibly talented Ousbach – thereafter to become a potter with works in the National Gallery – had by then also built a considerable reputation for dropping things.

One was a set of Georgian wine decanters that met their death when Anders tripped on the four steps going up (not down) to

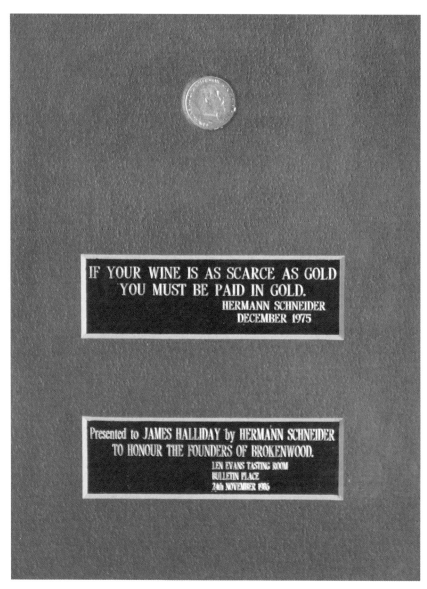

The framed gold sovereign and accompanying message from Hermann Schneider, of Two Faces Restaurant, the sovereign having the same value as the Brokenwood wine he purchased.

Evans's office at Bulletin Place. Another occurred while he was subsequently working as front of house at Hermann Schneider's revered Two Faces Restaurant in Melbourne. It was his day off, but he offered to come in to help at lunch; when my guests and I appeared on the top of the landing to the steps which led down to Two Faces, who should I find but Anders Ousbach, down on his knees trying to return some of the maraschino cherries to the two-kilo tin he had just dropped on the carpet. Pale faced at the best of times, his skin had the pallor of death as he looked up and blurted 'Oh god, not you.'

He was also a calligraphic artist in his own time and for his own pleasure, as we learnt at one Monday Options lunch. Evans's first series of questions led to the identification of the wine as Chateau Lafite. But try as we could we could not guess the vintage, which was surprising given that one of the recent great wine dinners at Bulletin Place (each featuring multiple vintages of a great wine) was of Chateau Lafite. Our exasperation reached boiling point, and rather than prolong the questions, Evans directed Anders to bring the bottle to the table. There it was: 1921 Chateau Lafite, but Evans had denied '21 as the vintage. He pointed again to the label: we saw it was 1921+, and milliseconds thereafter that the entire label, with its engraved depiction of the Chateau and nearby oak trees, plus its vintage in red, had been hand-drawn by Anders. The wine was a composite of all the great vintages between 1921 and 1961 that had been served at the great wine dinner, utilising the residue of each wine after it was decanted. It was a ritual Evans used with great success at subsequent dinners.

So, to return to the dinner, a sudden crash of glass announced that a bottle had fallen to the wooden floor. We all froze in shocked silence: with split-second timing Anders said, 'Shall we have the

A Life in Wine

1728, sir?' He had deliberately dropped an empty bottle, knowing full well what we would think.

It was not too long before he became one of us diners, and I shall never forget the night he wore battery-operated mock-diamond dress shirt buttons, which flashed on and off on command. I fancy it may have been another dinner attended by Fraser; certainly Evans had launched into his welcome speech when the flashing studs captured his attention. I rarely saw him caught out, but he was that night. He didn't know whether to ignore them (difficult, since we had all realised what was happening), laugh or become angry. In the end he did all three more or less simultaneously; the studs did not reappear at later dinners.

I was also the subject of one of Anders' practical jokes. He was at the time front of house at Gaye Bilson's Berowra Waters restaurant. It had a strict policy of no BYO, but it was possible to get around this by arranging delivery of your wines in advance (and on the basis that neither they nor anything similar was on the wine list). It was my birthday, and one of the wines was an unusually robust 1947 Fleurie (from Beaujolais) which ought to have gone to its grave but hadn't. (I purchased it from Christie's in a lot which also included a 1928 Fleurie bottled in Scotland by Matthew Gloag and Sons with the words 'A famous vintage' on its label; it, too, was amazingly good, making one wonder how much pinot noir was making its way into Beaujolais back then.)

When the time came to have the '47, Ousbach brought it to the table, presented it, opened it, and began to decant it. He broke off, saying, 'Oh dear; you had better have a look at this', giving me a small pour. It was vile: both oxidised and vinegary. 'Don't worry; we have a similar wine which I am sure you will find acceptable.' It was brought to the table already decanted, and was impeccable.

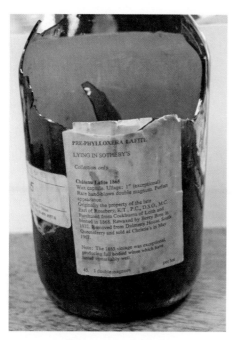

PRE-PHYLLOXERA LAFITE
LYING IN SOTHEBY'S

Collection only

Château Lafite 1865
Wax capsule. Ullage: 1" (exceptional)
Rare hand-blown double magnum. Perfect
appearance.
Originally the property of the late
Earl of Rosebery, K.T., P.C., D.S.O., M.C.
Purchased from Cockburns of Leith and
binned in 1868. Removed by Berry Bros in
1931. Removed from Dalmeny House, South
Queensferry and sold at Christie's in May
1967.

Note: The 1865 vintage was exceptional,
producing full bodied wines which have
lasted remarkably well.

45   1 double magnum   per lot

A tragedy: the remains of the (accidentally broken) double magnum of 1865 Chateau Lafite

My then wife Liz and I were seated at the end of the restaurant nearest the kitchen; a birthday surprise came when the dessert was served by a gorgeously statuesque 'waitress' dressed only in a pinafore tied around her waist. It all happened so quickly that no one else in the restaurant noticed it, except for one bloke at the other end, who sat transfixed with his fork halfway to his mouth, clearly disbelieving his eyes. (It turned out she was a friend of Gaye's and had been persuaded to do her bit for my birthday.) His attempts to persuade his fellow diners that he had seen a naked woman serving a table were equally amusing.

When the bill came, I noticed that there was no charge for the wine from Berowra Waters' cellar. When I insisted on paying, Anders came clean. He had decanted my bottle in advance, and refilled it with cooking wine spiked with vinegar, and with the skill of a counterfeiter, had replaced the cork and capsule so cleverly that they appeared untouched.

Ousbach was, by definition, a difficult person to present with a birthday present. John Parkinson, like Anders, at one stage worked

ABOVE: *My lifelong friend Michael Hornibrook and I were both born in 1938, and jointly celebrated our 'big' birthdays.*

BELOW: *Author (left) with Tony Albert and his wife Gayshe Albert.*

at Bulletin Place, and was one of the founders of the *Wine & Spirit Buying Guide*. He came up with a great idea: buy a flagon of Mick Morris' pre-phylloxera muscat, a treacle-thick and incredibly luscious wine used in tiny amounts in the oldest solera barrels of Morris' greatest muscat show wines.

It took Parkinson considerable time and effort to persuade Mick Morris to part with a flagon of this elixir; it was so rare as to be beyond price. But Morris finally yielded, and the flagon was presented. A month later Parkinson called in to check how the flagon was faring, and indicated he would appreciate a small taste. Anders didn't stammer, but his speech could be slightly hesitant, and Parkinson at first thought nothing of it when Anders hesitated.

But it became clear that there was a problem. A ghastly thought crossed Parkinson's mind: 'You didn't drop it, did you?' 'No,' came the answer, but the answer still took some time. Eventually Ousbach explained that he liked to sip it while he was reading in bed at night, but had found the process somewhat cumbersome given the tiny amount required for each taste.

He had mentioned the problem to a friend who was a male nurse, who immediately came up with the answer. He 'borrowed' a transfusion assembly from the hospital where he worked, and slung the flagon where the blood or saline bag would normally be positioned. Instead of a needle, the tube ended with a suction device, and Ousbach was able to sip on demand without interrupting his reading. One fateful night he fell asleep and had a profoundly erotic dream. Alas, when he awoke in the morning, the sheets were saturated and the flagon was empty. It had been the ultimate nocturnal experience.

Once again, I come back to the first dinner, and to the Old Wine Tasting. While it is impossible to repeat my tasting notes for all of the dinners (and even the menus), I have to admit that the 1727 Rudesheimer, while drinkable, had as much to do with fino sherry as it did table wine. The great Tun (or vat) in which the wine is still held has been topped up over the centuries as wine has evaporated or been drawn off, and it is anybody's guess how much the 1727 component represents.

On the other hand, there is no such doubt about the oldest wine to be served at a Single Bottle Club dinner, a 1646 Tokaji which, like the Rudesheimer, had been purchased from Christie's. It came in an onion-shaped but flat-bottomed pale duck egg blue striated glass bottle with a narrow neck and a tiny cork. Holding around 300ml, the bottle had obviously spent a century or more standing up, for the wine had precisely stained the interior of the neck to a level about 2mm above the level when it was opened.

While the wine had lost a lot of its sweetness, and may not have started its life as an essence, it had far more vinosity, strength and life than the Rudesheimer. Tragically, my car was broken into a few days after the dinner and my briefcase (containing the menu, wine list and my tasting notes) was stolen. The contents likely ended up on a council rubbish tip somewhere.

But Len Evans had the bottle, and on his death it passed into my possession. There are other copies of the menu, of which I have one, and I remember how this piece of living history – made while Cromwell was stalking the fields of England – tasted.

Enough. The wines which followed the Rudesheimer were 1898 Chateau Villemaurine (St Emilion), 1894 Chateau Ausone (St Emilion), 1893 Chateau Lafite (the first great vintage after phylloxera), 1878 Chateau Peyrabon (Haut Medoc), 1874 Chateau Lafite (along with 1875, the last great vintage before phylloxera), 1872 Craiglee Sunbury Hermitage, 1825 Chateau Gruaud-Larose (an excellent vintage, coming directly from the Chateau via Michael Broadbent's hand luggage, and inevitably cloudy, but still great, and the oldest Bordeaux I have tasted) and, to finish, 1888 Chateau d'Yquem.

The following year, at a dinner held on 25 September, the decision was made to focus on younger wines which were acknowledged classics thanks to a combination of breed and vintage. The menus, printed in gold on a black leather-coated hardboard square, doubled as placemats. At the last moment, the Prime Minister was detained by affairs of state, and famously sent his driver to collect his menu (each had our name on it) – he was (infamously or apocryphally) believed to have driven from Canberra to do so.

In short order, the wines were 1947 Pol Roger, 1947 Veuve Clicquot (magnum), 1959 Le Montrachet (Marquis de Laguiche) (magnum), 1952 Batard Montrachet (magnum), 1953 Chateau Lafite, 1949 Chateau Mouton-Rothschild, 1947 Chateau Cheval Blanc, 1945 Chateau Latour, 1929 Chateau Lafite, 1871 Chateau Gruaud-Larose, 1955 Chambertin (Leroy), 1953 Corton (Hospices de Beaune) (magnum) and 1921 Clos de la Roche (Barolet) (yes, again, but it was then at the peak of its form). Then three Trockenbeerenausleses: 1976 Berncastler Doktor (Thanisch) and 1971 and 1959 Wehlener Sonnenuhr (JJ Prum). Two classic vintage ports rounded off the night: 1927 Croft and 1908 Cockburn.

Well, not quite. The Mouton and Latour were exceptional bottles of supremely great wines, but at the end of the night I cruised the table pouring the remnants of the three Trockenbeerenausleses into my three glasses. Wines of this intensity and concentration from the Mosel come only in the greatest vintages, and then in microquantities – as little as 10 dozen in total. These days most are sold at special auctions in Germany, bringing a thousand or so dollars a bottle.

The black leather menu doubled as a placemat.

Regardless, I have no regrets about my unseemly behaviour: that utterly magical combination of lime-blossom sweetness, balanced by crystal-pure lemony acidity, lasting a full minute or more after each sip, did not deserve to be wasted.

1980 marked Len Evans's 50th birthday, and, quite properly, a number of dinners were held in celebration. The Single Bottle Club dinner was held on 9 September; 1930 was a woeful vintage, but the

Chateau Petrus Dinner　　　　　　　　*Wednesday, September 10th, 1980*

GAME TERRINE	1976 CHATEAU PETRUS
	1975 CHATEAU PETRUS
	1971 CHATEAU PETRUS
	1970 CHATEAU PETRUS
	1966 CHATEAU PETRUS
FEUILLETTE of LAMB'S BRAINS with	1964 CHATEAU PETRUS
TRUFFLE SAUCE	1962 CHATEAU PETRUS
	1961 CHATEAU PETRUS
SALAD of PIGEON BREAST & PICKLED WALNUTS	1959 CHATEAU PETRUS
	1957 CHATEAU PETRUS
	1955 CHATEAU PETRUS
	1953 CHATEAU PETRUS
ESCALOPES of SWEETBREADS on BRIOCHE with	1952 CHATEAU PETRUS
CEPE SAUCE	1949 CHATEAU PETRUS
	1948 CHATEAU PETRUS
	1947 CHATEAU PETRUS
Pear & Pink Peppercorn Sorbet	
	1945 CHATEAU PETRUS
SADDLE of HARE with RED WINE DEMI-GLACE	1943 CHATEAU PETRUS
	1926 CHATEAU PETRUS
GOAT'S CHEESE	1919 CHATEAU PETRUS

Guest Chef: Gregory Doyle

The greatest Chateau Petrus dinner ever staged in Australia.

wine list included four wines of that year: Chateau Lanessan, Beaune Clos des Mouches, Yalumba Port and Seppelt Port. The only wine made after 1950 was a vibrant bottle of '62 Penfolds Bin 60A, one of the greatest Australian red wines, and then only 18 years old; now it is still superb, albeit with increasing bottle variation.

The highlights were 1909 Hope Valley Burgundy (made in Coonawarra by Bill Redman for D.A. Tolley), another 1872 Craiglee Sunbury, more '21 d'Yquem and Marc Bredif Vouvray Liquoreux, and the crescendo of the 1646 Tokaji – liquid history.

The next night, 10 September, it was Len Evans's turn to stage a dinner designed to put all others in the box: 20 vintages of Chateau Petrus from 1976 back to 1919, with all the greatest vintages of '45, '47, '48, '49, '53, '61 and '66. Obligatory champagnes started the dinner, d'Yquems finished it.

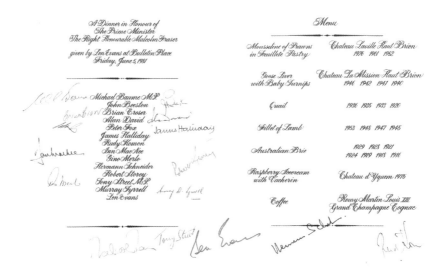

The 5 June 1981 dinner, with Prime Minister Malcolm Fraser as guest of honour, featured 19 vintages of Chateau La Mission Haut Brion

The Petrus dinner marked a change in the Single Bottle Club format. From this point on we chose a theme, or themes; the host also rotated (the host paid for the dinner and menus). Thus on 5 June 1981, Len Evans was host, and the Prime Minister the guest of honour. The wine theme was Chateau La Mission Haut Brion, with 19 vintages spread between 1916 and 1947. We started with three vintages of its sister white wine, Chateau Laville Haut Brion ('76, '61 and '52), and finished with '75 Chateau d'Yquem and Remy Martin Louis XIII Cognac.

Persistence paid off, for the following year we headed off to the Prime Minister's Lodge in Canberra. Fraser had telephoned Len from London to check whether a '65 Chateau Lafite would be suitable as his wine. A major diplomatic incident was averted by an intake of breath from Evans (1965 was a woeful year in Bordeaux) and a pregnant pause, allowing the Prime Minister to add '1865, of course'. Evans gravely assented, for – after all – this is one of the very greatest of pre-phylloxera vintages.

The most interesting bracket (by far, after the splendour of the Lafite) was the last: 1921 Forster Jesuitengarten Trockenbeerenauslese (from the Rhinepfalz), 1901 Tokaji 5 puttonyos, 1892 Chateau d'Yquem, 1890 Falernian (a swindle, but a comic Italian one, we concluded), 1815 Duke of Wellington Malaga, and 1791 Constantia (from South Africa's Cape of Good Hope) – the last two as magnificent as they were historic.

A Life in Wine

ABOVE: *The Brokenwood gardener and odd jobs man (author) at work.*
BELOW: *The forklift attached to the tractor required a jury-rigged counterweight on the back, the safety officer (author) inspecting.*

CHAPTER 8

EUROPEAN SOJOURNS
1979–85

In 1979 I had participated in the vintage activities of Len Evans's two Chateaux in Bordeaux: Chateau Rahoul in Graves (dry red) and Chateau Padouen in Sauternes, the latter a particularly memorable experience as we dissected the already-harvested bunches with pairs of nail scissors, separating the botrytised berries from the unaffected, and (with Brian Croser directing) Padouen made two wines, one a dry white Bordeaux, the other a full-on Sauternes. Cutting up the bunches caused clouds of mould spores to fill the room, to the extent that we had to periodically suspend operations and take a walk in the courtyard.

OPPOSITE: *Lunch on the verandah at Brokenwood. Author in the foreground, looking quizzical.*

On one memorable day off from vintage, we drove down to Michel Guerard's three-star restaurant Eugenie-Les-Bains for lunch. The group, with Len Evans at the head, included Primo Caon (Adelaide restaurateur), Gino Merlo (then one of Brisbane's leading restaurateurs), Brian Croser and myself. It was a no-holds-barred lunch, and we rolled out around 4pm and headed due west to the coast and Biarritz.

Our destination there was the then two-star Café de Paris, which had a fabulous wine list. Evans being Evans, he insisted on a visit to the casino on the way to dinner, where a patrician gentleman in a white tuxedo soon attached himself to us, intent – so it appeared – on asking us to dinner. Quite what he hoped to achieve was not clear, but Evans was onto him in a flash. Almost 20 years earlier, the man had been a celebrated confidence trickster who had attempted to ply his trade in the Silver Spade Room at the Chevron Hilton in Kings Cross, during Evans's time as food and beverage manager of the hotel.

Needless to say, we went to dinner without his patronage, although I seem to remember he followed us to the Café de Paris and sat alone, without any sign of defeat or embarrassment. Our plan that night was to have the bare minimum of food – a salad followed by steak and frites – and the maximum of wine. The wines chosen all came from the great vintages of the 1920s and 1940s, all from celebrated estates in Bordeaux and Burgundy (we didn't deem to stoop to the Rhône Valley).

The evening was long, the wines many, and we at last arrived at a small dessert and the 'stickies'. Having ordered (and consumed) what we thought was necessary, the need for another bottle of Sauternes became apparent. As it was brought to our table, the entire staff in the restaurant gathered behind the rail that separated a slightly higher floor from the one we were on, and applauded us. We, for our part, would have applauded them had we known that the bill for the food was exactly the same as that for the wine: all we knew as we went along was that the wines were absurdly cheap.

It was a situation I was to encounter on many occasions over the ensuing few years, brought about by French tax law, which said that if the value of trading stock was increased by more than a small amount (perhaps the measure of inflation) each year, tax had to be paid on all the increase regardless of whether the stock (in this instance, the wine) had been sold. Since price rises for current vintages ex the producers had risen at a substantially greater rate, and (I strongly suspect) annual price adjustments caused too much book-keeping work, the prices for current vintage wines were not infrequently greater than those of wines 30 or 40 years older. The French penchant for drinking wines when young also played a part in this.

In 1982 I had the opportunity to explore this phenomenon extensively. While Clayton Utz had introduced a two-month sabbatical leave every three years in the early 1970s, my temporary abscondment to merchant banking in the mid '70s meant that my turn was late in coming, and I was determined to enjoy it to its fullest. My wife-to-be Suzanne had departed several months before me to learn French, and we met in Champagne. For many years before (and after) 1982 I had helped judge the annual champagne competition funded by the CIVC (Comité Interprofessionel du Vins de Champagne), and we were the guests of the champagne houses for over a week of non-stop champagne drinking.

The exchange rate was very favourable, and fine dining was amazingly cheap. As we exited south from Champagne, Suzanne and I were to embark on a 12-day period in which we ate at 13 three-star restaurants, the bookings having been made on our behalf (but at our cost, naturally) by the CIVC. The trifecta came with successive meals at Auberge du Père Bise at Talloires (now only one-star) on Saturday night, Le Pyramide at Vienne for Sunday lunch, and Troisgros at Roanne on Sunday night.

In each instance we had booked accommodation in the restaurant premises, and (incredible though it now seems) dinner, bed and breakfast averaged $150 for the two of us.

Our introduction to Auberge du Père Bise did not begin well. We arrived as lunch was underway, simply wanting to confirm our booking and ascertain whether or not our room was ready. We left our Renault A5 parked in the driveway. When it appeared that there was no booking, a minor stand-off developed, and 'Madame' had to be summoned, her initial concern being our humble car disrupting traffic.

It transpired that we did indeed have a reservation for a table that night, but we had been booked in at a large old hotel on the side of the lake at Talloires. Ruffled feathers (on both sides) smoothed, we moved the offending A5 down to the hotel. We returned in time for a half bottle of champagne in the garden adjacent to the restaurant, and had nearly finished when Madame arrived to inform me that Kit Stevens MW (Master of Wine) was on the phone wishing to speak to me. (He was my contact for many of the wines I was buying in those days as a consultant for David Jones.)

When I returned, another half bottle of champagne had arrived courtesy of Madame, it being obvious that Kit had persuaded her I was a person of importance. Moving to dinner, we decided to start with a bottle of sauternes, drinking half with foie gras, saving the other half for dessert. Bottles of white and red burgundy followed, then the other half of the sauternes. Some evil spirit then persuaded me that we should have an additional half bottle of sauternes to help the consumption of the rich dessert we had chosen.

ABOVE: *A view of the back courtyard of our house in Monthelie, Burgundy, with adjoining backyard.*
BELOW: *The front courtyard entrance of our Monthelie house. The white door at the bottom leads to an underground cellar.*

Madame was now sure that we were worthy customers, and insisted we should each have a glass of 1938 Armagnac. Two very large glasses were duly produced. I drank mine, and lurched off to the loo. When I returned, Madame was sitting with Suzanne, who had switched her full glass for my empty one prior to Madame's return to the table. 'Don't you like my Armagnac?' asked Madame, and there was, of course, only one answer.

Back at the hotel, I very briefly lay on the bed and closed my eyes before the world began to spin around me, a situation I knew, from my university days, was a precursor to violent illness. I moved to the vast marble-floored bathroom, and sat on the edge of the bath, strategically adjacent to the toilet. Five or so hours later I awoke, lying on my side on the cold marble floor, with a laser drilling a hole in my right eye, and Alfred Hitchcock birds screeching outside the window.

I crawled into bed for a few more hours' sleep, and got up feeling seriously sick. We were due at Le Pyramide in Vienne for lunch, and I knew that if I were a passenger, frequent roadside stops would be necessary. As I drove, I kept mumbling a litany of regret about my inability to do justice to the fabulous wine list, and probably the lunch itself.

I had made a partial recovery by the time we arrived and walked past Fernand Point's widow, seated as ever in a small office looking into the vestibule, greeting regular customers. One of these, a lady of comparable age to the widow, had a small dog that sat on a chair at the table of its mistress, and delicately ate its lunch off the plate in front of it.

The menu and wine list arrived. The former was quickly disposed of: since positive choice betokened an active desire for one dish or another, it had to be the Menu Gastronomique. The wine list was another matter, and rapidly dispelled any idea of a single bottle. There was a '38 Louis Latour Corton Charlemagne and a '38 Domaine de la Romanée-Conti, with an all-up cost of 2100 francs for the two bottles and Menu Gastronomique for two, or $350 at the then rate of exchange.

When I had smelt the check pour of the Romanée-Conti Suzanne asked me why I was crying. I indignantly replied that I was not, whereupon she suggested I touch my cheeks. Sure enough, there were unbidden tears of joy at the perfection of the wine. The vintage was dreadful in Bordeaux, but good in Champagne, the Loire Valley and Burgundy, quite apart from being my birth year.

Over the next two years I returned several times to La Pyramide, methodically draining the cellar first of Romanée-Conti, then of La Tache, and making a determined assault on the Domaine's Richebourg before the collapse of the Australian dollar. I gazed wistfully at the dozen or so bottles of 1806 Chateau Lafite still in the cellar – they had been available for a derisory amount until a bottle was sold at a US auction for a very large sum, whereupon it was hurriedly removed from the wine list. (In 1951, Lafite sold parcels of its 1806 vintage to a number of three-star restaurants in a rather curious promotional exercise.)

Returning to that Sunday, we went on to Troisgros at Roanne for our evening meal. I was known by the brothers Troisgros as a result of a visit to Australia by one of them, and we were ushered into the kitchen to watch the preparation of the evening's dishes, and smell the assorted scents and aromas of the food – not strictly necessary as far as I was concerned. Nor were the successive arrivals of various amuse bouche.

Once again, positive food selection was impossible, so we defaulted to the degustation menu. On returning to the dining room, we found our adjoining table occupied by a young American couple. In accordance with a long-set protocol, we kept our voices as low as possible in the hope that they would not hear us speaking English, and thus not regale us with a short history of their lives and likes. All went well until I let the cat out of the bag, and they immediately pounced.

'We have spent the last day preparing for this wonderful restaurant and this wonderful meal,' intoned he. 'We only had a light breakfast' (I was momentarily tempted to ask what that might have been given the normal American gargantuan pile of waffles, maple syrup, hash browns, crispy bacon, scrambled eggs and more heaped onto their plates) 'and we skipped lunch, just drinking juice and water. We knew this was the only way we could really enjoy tonight.' And so it went on, with grunts of assent from Suzanne and I.

Both then and subsequently I wondered what they would have said about the finer points of our preparation, but concluded that they would be sure we were escapees from a lunatic asylum.

Much later in the same trip, we had planned a return visit to the Café de Paris, again using Bordeaux as our launch pad, leaving after a pre-arranged lunch at Chateau Palmer. We had dined at Bordeaux's best restaurant, St James, the previous night, and by the following morning it was painfully clear that I was suffering from a mild attack (if there is such a thing) of food poisoning. The lunch at Chateau Palmer – a magret de canard and 1959 Chateau Palmer – was frequently broken by my sprints to the toilet, as unfortunate for the late Peter Sichel (our host) as for me.

Our trip to Biarritz was in the company of Brenton Fry, general manager of Negociants (Yalumba's import/export business); the three of us were on our way back to Burgundy, and he was unconvinced that the circuitous route (turning one day's drive into two long ones) was merited by the Café de Paris. As we drove south, so was I; while emergency stops became less frequent, I was still feeling appalling.

We arrived in Biarritz, checked into our hotel and took a lengthy walk around the cliffs. For some obscure reason, the image of the giant European black and gold bee feeding on wild flowers remains imprinted on my mind. So, too, is the course of events at the dinner: as we were seated, and I looked again at the wine list, I suddenly felt well again. Perhaps it was the reception we were accorded on our arrival. The staff all remembered the visit of the crazy Australians in 1979; Len Evans, too, had (separately) returned, and was also greeted like a long-lost friend.

The white burgundies had never been a strong point, but a 1964 Beaune Clos de Mouche was a good enough start. I had then chosen 1962 Domaine de la Romanée-Conti La Tache and Richebourg to compare with each other. 1962 La Tache was the most important vinous milestone of my life. It was served to me by Len Evans at his Greenwich home not long after we had become friends in 1968; while still a young wine, I had never experienced anything like it. It marked the beginning of a love affair with Burgundy and Domaine de la Romanée-Conti which remains undiminished. (It is thus doubly appropriate that I should be writing these words in the house in Monthelie, Burgundy, which a group of us purchased in 1998.)

Having chosen two such great Burgundies, I hesitated about the choice of the third red wine (for the cheese) but settled on 1955 Chateau la Mission Haut Brion, to be followed by 1950 Chateau d'Yquem. Not long thereafter, the sommelier returned 'desolée'; there was indeed no more Richebourg, but he did have a bottle of 1962 Romanée-Conti without a label (but with a branded cork, naturally). Would we be happy with this at the same price as the Richebourg? We were indeed.

When it came time for dessert, Suzanne declined to participate, and Brenton and I found the act of choice as difficult as I had at Troisgros. 'Never mind, it's easy,' said our waiter. Shortly thereafter 13 small plates were placed in a semi-circle in front of both Brenton and myself. I still feel he was guilty of bad manners in not eating them all; I had to defend the honour of Australia. I do have to admit, however, that as we set off in drizzling rain the following day for the long drive to Burgundy, I was glad to be driving rather than sitting in the rear seat.

In September/October 1983 I became a vintage cellar rat at Domaine Dujac, the highly regarded Morey-St-Denis winery owned by Jacques and Ros Seysses. By sheer coincidence, and unknown to each other, Gary Farr of Bannockburn (in Geelong) had also signed on for his first vintage. We both learnt a tremendous amount, and he returned year after year, which was more than I could manage. I also absconded for two special-purpose overnight trips to Le Pyramide to continue my attack on its cellar of '38 DRCs, and for a week-long trip to the Douro, my hosts including the Van Zeller family of Quinta do Noval, the Symingtons (of many of the best known brands) and the Cockburns.

We had two Single Bottle Club Dinners in 1983, one before, the other after, my sojourn in Burgundy. Murray Tyrrell and Len Evans were hosts at the 25 May 1983 dinner in honour of the memory of Rudy Komon, the leading art dealer and eminence gris in all matters vinous, who had been a member of the Single Bottle Club since its inception, and who had died not long previously.

It was the only all-Australian dinner for the Club, and featured an array of Australian classics which would be nigh-on impossible to source today. The youngest of the ten white wines were from '56, the oldest '37; the first red bracket was five Seppelt Great Western wines made by Colin Preece between '49 and '54; the second red bracket started with '53 Grange and finished – triumphantly – with '39 Mount Pleasant Mountain C and '37 Mount Pleasant Mountain A made by Maurice O'Shea. Preece and O'Shea are legends, and each would have been delighted with his wines.

The dinner finished with Lindemans Porphyry from '56, '49 and '37, but the menu designed by Len Evans was pure Australiana: Sydney Harbour Stew, Pigeon Livers in Pastry, Saddle of Mutton with vegetables, Cheese and Chocolate Flan.

With leading (then) Brisbane restaurateur Gino Merlo as host and the much bemedalled Governor of Queensland (and his ADC) in attendance, the second dinner of the 1983 year, on 23 November, was the first all Burgundy dinner (excepting '76 and '71 Krug to commence, and '61 Chateau d'Yquem, '47 Chateau Lafaurie Peraguey plus more Louis XIII Cognac to finish).

There were 27 wines in all (the single bottle per person had long since become a nominal count). A 1923 Chassagne Montrachet from Alix Vigneau (a shipper) just outpointed 1972 Le Montrachet (DRC), which was golden hued and honeyed. The big guns fired with '69 and '62 Romanée-Conti, the ubiquitous '48 La Tache, '43 La Tache, '43 Richebourg (DRC), '34 Chambolle Musigny (Barolet) and '20 Corton (Hospices de Beaune Cuvee Charlotte Dumay).

The '62 Romanée-Conti (unbelievable power, grace and elegance) got the perfect score from me, 20/20 or, if you wish, 100/100, with the '43 Richebourg not far behind, all finesse and freshness. The one partial disappointment was the '69 Romanée-Conti, which was complex enough, but with a slight pencil shavings character, probably from the cork.

Having participated in two vintages in 1983, I decided to take a vintage holiday in 1984. However, this did not mean I turned my

A Dinner in the honour of
the late Rudy Komon MBE
a member of the Single Bottle Club
given by Murray Tyrrell and Len Evans OBE
at Bulletin Place
Wednesday, May 25, 1983

Tony Albert
Michael Baume
John Beston
Primo Caon
Brian Croser
David Farmer
The Right Honourable Malcolm Fraser CH
James Halliday
Frances Henry
Ian Macrae
Gene Merb
Sir John Mason KCMG
Hermann Schneider
Robert Story
Tony Struel MP
Murray Tyrrell
Len Evans OBE

Menu

	Seppelt Great Western Sparkling Burgundy	1946
	Seppelt Great Western Show Champagne	1954
Sydney Harbour Stew	Great Western Chablis M14	1956
	Tullochs Hunter River Semillon	1956
	Tullochs Hunter River Semillon	1954
	Mount Pleasant Verona Riesling	1953
	Mount Pleasant Light Dry White 54/55 J	1953
Pigeon Livers in Pastry	Great Western Riesling Tokay	1959
	Orlando Barossa Riesling	1953
	Seppelt Riesling	1956
	Rhinecastle Rhine Riesling Bin 104	1945
	Yalumba Eden Valley Rhine Riesling S22	1941
Saddle of Mutton with Vegetables	Great Western Claret KM	1954
	Great Western Burgundy Q13	1953
	Great Western Claret TM	1951
	Great Western Claret A 66/33	1951
	Great Western Burgundy P30/34	1949
Cheese	Penfolds Grange Hermitage	1953
	Rhinecastle Victorian Burgundy Bin 23	1952
	Rhinecastle Burgundy Bin 25	1949
	Mount Pleasant Mountain C Dry Red	1939
	Mount Pleasant Mountain A Dry Red	1937
Chocolate Flan	Lindemans Porphyry	1956
	Lindemans Porphyry	1949
	Lindemans Porphyry	1937

An exceptional dinner of great classic Australian wines.

back on wine. I made numerous visits to the Yarra Valley, making myself more familiar with the (informal) sub-regions and their characteristics. I had also begun planning for the 1985 vintage, which would be my first in the Valley, and made arrangements to purchase grapes from four vineyards in the Valley, while sourcing small-scale winemaking equipment.

I also continued with my annual pilgrimage to France, concentrating on the Loire Valley, Rhône Valley and Burgundy, where I purchased wines for David Jones Connoisseurs' Wine Club, with help and advice from Kit Stevens, who arranged visits and often accompanied me. He had lived in Cognac for some years, and had also maintained a garret office on the fifth floor of a building in Paris, reached without the aid of a lift.

A Life in Wine

Needless to say, his French was fluent (and mine abysmal), but he always seemed happier speaking in English to the locals. On one occasion we were trying to find Domaine Berger in Montlouis, a small town in the Loire Valley, driving around in circles. After a while, we (Suzanne was with me) suggested he ask someone for directions. 'No,' came Kit's response, 'they are all fools.' Unwillingly, he ultimately stopped and asked whether the whereabouts of Domaine Berger was known, and no help was forthcoming. 'See,' cried Kit triumphantly, 'I told you so.' Further circumnavigation of the village proving fruitless, other than in terms of increasingly curious stares, there was no alternative than to stop once again. The question 'Where is Domaine Berger?' was met (once again) with a shrug of the shoulders and denial of knowledge.

This caused Kit to lose his temper, insisting that it was in this town – and nearby – whereupon the local responded 'Ah, Domaine Berger', placing an infinitesimally different emphasis on the 'ger', and pointing to the opposite side of the street, said, 'C'est là.' We were, in fact, directly opposite our destination. 'I told you they are fools,' Kit proclaimed, as we tried unsuccessfully to quell our convulsive laughter.

I, however, suffered the same fate 20 years later, when stranded in Beaune by Suzanne and instructed to catch a non-existent taxi back to our house in Monthelie. As I was walking past Pommard, a sudden change in the weather ended the sunshine, an icy wind began to blow as the temperature plummeted, and I watched helplessly as a curtain of rain approached.

By now I was on the gradual ascent up to Volnay, and as anyone who had driven on that road will know, there is no shelter except for a curious Cave de Crus stone building all on its own (usually unoccupied) and a large tree in front. By now my shirt (I had no jumper)

The Noble Grape

A Life in Wine

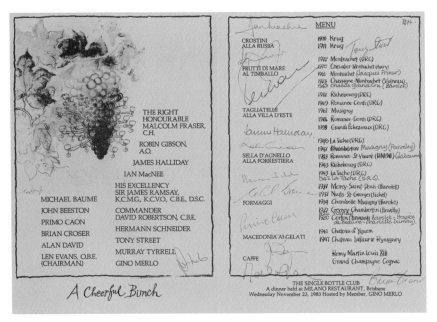

The Italian blood in host Gino Merlo meant numerous extempore changes to the menu.

was drenched, and I stopped to take cover. Within a very short time I was on my way again, having discovered that I was likely to freeze to death unless I kept moving.

As I breasted the top of the Volnay hill, almost within sight of the large Monthelie sign, a car stopped and the driver motioned for me to get in. He asked me (in French) where I was going, and I answered 'Monthelie'. He looked puzzled, so I repeated the name. Still no light dawned, so I motioned for him to drive on. Several hundred metres later the sign came into view, and I pointed to it. 'Ah, Monthelie,' he said, with that same sliding accent on the last syllable which had been necessary for the identification of Berger. Matters clarified, he insisted on driving me to the front door of our house, before departing with a friendly smile and wave.

CHAPTER 9

SIGNS OF THINGS TO COME
1975–85

The high point of red wine sales in Australia had come in 1974/75; it was the last year in which its sales were greater than those of white wine. 1974 was a cornerstone year for many reasons. It was the year in which the Trade Practices Act was passed, making retail price fixing illegal, although the breweries held firm on pricing for another four years (they were still the dominant sales route for wine). It was the year in which the last of the technical problems for the wine cask were solved. It also marked the time at which the major retail chains became interested in wine, beer and spirits retailing.

Kevin McLintock, then chief executive of McWilliams Wines, also nominated 1975 as the crossover point from colonial to continental influence on lifestyle, measured not so much in terms of wine

---

OPPOSITE: *The author just emerged from waist-deep immersion in red ferment, Brokenwood 1975.*

consumption as on that of coffee (on the ascendant) and tea (on the descendent).

Guenter Prass, then head of Orlando, put his stamp on the decade when he wrote: 'I remember the first discount I came across: in 1978, a discount of five cents per four-litre cask to Tooth Wine and Spirits in Sydney for the supply of five semi-trailers of cask wine.' In an odd foretaste of the decades to come, a major story on the wine industry in the *Bulletin* magazine began with the words 'Savage discounting of wine has become the ultimate marketing folly for the Australian wine industry. What began as a means of carving out a market share has turned into a deadly war of survival for the country's 300-odd wine producers.' Plus ça change.

At the start of the 1970s, bottles had 48 per cent of the market, flagons 40 per cent, casks 2 per cent and bulk/fill-your-own 10 per cent. By 1985 the share of bottled wine had halved to 24 per cent, flagons had a (still falling) share of 9 per cent, casks had a (still rising) share of 65 per cent, bulk a negligible but falling 2 per cent.

In 1983 Wayne Jackson (then chief executive of Thomas Hardy) addressed the NSW Wine Press Club:

The cask has played a key role and is indeed a catalyst and vehicle for the rampant price competition currently existing and worsening in the Australian wine industry. The relevance and ultimate effect of this insanity on the profitability, and even viability, of winemaking companies is surely obvious to us all.

Since the early 1970s when the softpack first was introduced to Australia – and I am deliberately excluding the original 'tin can' – there have been no less than 32 major takeovers and share-acquisitions of winemaking companies in Australia. I contend that lack of an adequate return on funds invested in the industry has been in part brought about by the nil or negative contribution which softpacks make to the net bottom line. This has been a major contributing factor to these takeovers.

Since 2000 the aggressive building of Liquorland/ Vintage Cellars (Coles Myer) and Safeway/First Estate (Woolworths) has caused much comment and concern. Yet during 1981 and the early part of 1982 GJ Coles (then still to merge with Myer) acquired 54 Claude Fay stores (a chain itself created since the late '70s), 14 Liquorland stores and the Colonial Cellars chain, all in Sydney. By April 1982 Myer already had 90 outlets across the country, having purchased the San Remo and Crittenden stores in Melbourne. In a familiar role, Woolworths was playing catch up, with 35 stores in New South Wales.

The effect on total wine consumption was dramatic: it more than doubled from 8.7 litres per capita in 1970 to 18.2 litres per capita in 1980, going on to peak at 21.6 litres in 1986. Notwithstanding the imposition of a 10 per cent wholesale sales tax on wine in August 1984, doubled to 20 per cent in the August 1986 budget, increases in wine prices lagged way behind the CPI increase in every year between 1977/78 and 1986/87.

The imposition of tax was inevitable: prior to its introduction, cask wine was cheaper than lemonade or Coca-Cola, let alone beer. Falling beer consumption was denting budget receipts, and a wine tax was the obvious solution.

What had been good news for the consumer was bad news for the wine producers. Wayne Jackson pointed out that the January 1977 *Thomson's Liquor Guide* wholesale price for the largest-selling 4.5-litre wine cask was $4.50. Annual inflation was then running at higher than 10 per cent per annum, but if a lesser rate had been applied until 1983, the wholesale price should have been $8, the retail $11. In fact, in the week he addressed the Wine Press Club, Crown of the Hill Cellars (the then equivalent of Theo's or Kemeny's) was selling casks for $2.99.

The massive increase in sales in Australia between 1975 and 1985 was entirely driven by white wine, but not in the manner most would these days assume. In 1985 only 11,000 tonnes of chardonnay were crushed, compared with 46,000 tonnes of riesling, 36,000 tonnes of semillon; more importantly, more than half the total white grape crush used for winemaking was of non-premium grapes, muscat gordo blanco to the fore.

So, accepting that casks by now had a stranglehold on the overall market, what were the top ten selling bottled brands in 1985 (white, red or sparkling)? In descending order, they were Kaiser Stuhl Summer Wine, Seppelt Great Western Champagne, Leo Buring Liebfrauwine,

Lindemans Ben Ean, McWilliams Sparkling Bodega, Penfolds Minchinbury Champagne, Seaview Champagne, Miranda Golden Gate Spumante, Wolf Blass Rhine Riesling and Queen Adelaide Rhine Riesling. The wheels fell off the rampant sparkling wine sales within two years, but it reflects an extraordinarily different market from that of the new millennium.

(As at 30 June 2003 the list read, again in descending order, Jacob's Creek Chardonnay Pinot, Yellowglen Yellow Champagne [sic], Jacob's Creek Chardonnay, Queen Adelaide Chardonnay, Lindemans Bin 65 Chardonnay, Rosemount Chardonnay, Brown Brothers Crouchen & Riesling Moselle, Houghton White Burgundy, Jacob's Creek Shiraz Cabernet and Seaview Brut.)

Yet further problems for the industry lay in the imbalance between imports and exports. The latter were stagnant, the former were not. In its 1977 Annual Report, the Australian Wine Board said:

Imports of wine in the period 1970/71 to 1976/77 increased by 239 per cent ... The trend is continuing to concern the wine industry not only because of the possibility that some of these wines do not conform to Australian Regulations regarding additives and labelling, but also because of the implications for growth of Australian wine sales and the prosperity of the rural community they support ... The Board has requested State Ministers of Health to take steps to have the law enforced prohibiting the sale of products which do not meet the prescribed standards for wine set out in the relevant legislation.

As the Australian dollar rose to giddy heights, reaching then unprecedented levels against sterling and the US dollar, and as the abundant, high-quality Bordeaux vintages fed their way through the system, imports continued to increase.

As you will readily understand, while I was doing everything in my power to keep imports booming, they were to be rapidly made insignificant as the export boom of the second half of the 1980s got underway – and ended 25 years later. The scenario is an eerie prelude to the situation in 2011, and simply demonstrates the cyclical nature of trade balances and imbalances.

Chris Quirk, then Research Officer of the Australian Wine Board, wrote in 1980:

One of the most important developments on the Australian wine scene during the 1970s has been the industry's successful transition from what up to the sixties was in many ways a cottage industry to an integral part of the competitive consumer goods market.

How ironic, then, that by 2011 the industry was seeking to persuade both the domestic and export markets that its best wines are handmade in the finest traditions of cottage industries.

ABOVE: *Presentation of McCubbin triptych at the 25th birthday celebration of Brokenwood, October 1995.*
BELOW: *The McCubbin triptych itself. From left (centre panel), Lyn Beeston, John Beeston, Tony Albert and Liz Halliday on the first trip after buying the land in 1970, and before the bulldozer moved in.*

CHAPTER 10

DUAL RESIDENCE 1983–88

When Suzanne and I moved to Melbourne in mid 1983, we rented a house in Millswyn Street, South Yarra. It was my intention and expectation that we would stay there until mid 1988, when I would retire (for the last time) from Clayton Utz, just prior to my 50th birthday. I made no secret of my intentions; my partners took the view that while everyone would like to retire before they are 50, when the time came I wouldn't be able to afford it.

As if to soften the blow of the loss of Sydney as my home city, the Single Bottle Club came to Melbourne in 1984; Hermann Schneider was host at Two Faces on 17 August 1984, with predictably superb food to accompany an all-Bordeaux dinner. '53 Chateau

OPPOSITE:*Author with the late Judy Hirst, wife of Robert Hirst, CEO of Coldstream Hills' distribution company for a decade. Close inspection shows the stripes match.*

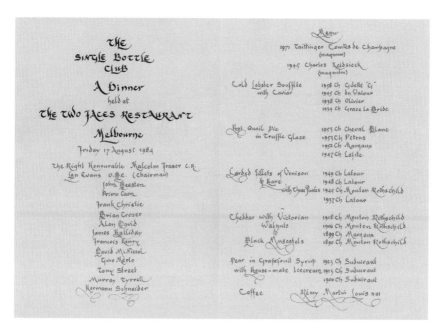

The handwritten menu reads:

THE
SINGLE BOTTLE
CLUB

A Dinner
held at
THE TWO FACES RESTAURANT

Melbourne

Friday 17 August 1984

The Right Honourable Malcolm Fraser C.H.
Len Evans O.B.E. (Chairman)
John Beeston
Primo Caon
Frank Christie
Brian Crozer
Alan David
James Halliday
Francois Kenny
David McNicol
Guno Merlo
Tony Street
Murray Tyrrell
Hermann Schneider

Menu

1971 Taittinger Comtes de Champagne
(magnum)
1945 Charles Heidsieck
(magnum)

Cold Lobster Soufflée   1958 Ch Gilette "C"
with Caviar   1945 Ch du Valour
                             1938 Ch Olivier
                             1934 Ch Grace La Bride

Hot Quail Pie   1953 Ch Cheval Blanc
in Truffle Glaze   1953 Ch Petrus
                            1952 Ch Margaux
                            1947 Ch Lafite

Larded Fillets of Venison   1949 Ch Latour
& Hare   1948 Ch Latour
            with Three Purées 1945 Ch Mouton Rothschild
                            1937 Ch Latour

Cheddar with Victorian   1918 Ch Mouton Rothschild
Walnuts   1906 Ch Mouton Rothschild
                            1899 Ch Margaux
Black Muscatels   1890 Ch Mouton Rothschild

Pear in Grapefruit Syrup   1923 Ch Suduiraut
with House-made Icecream   1913 Ch Suduiraut
                            1900 Ch Suduiraut

Coffee   Rémy Martin Louis XIII

Yet another dinner with Malcolm Fraser in attendance.

Cheval Blanc and '53 Chateau Petrus; '49, '48 and '37 Chateau
Latour; '45, '18, '06 and 1890 Chateau Mouton-Rothschild; '52
and 1899 Chateau Margaux (the latter a great vintage); and '23,
'13 and '00 Chateau Suduiraut for the dessert – plus another four
whites and magnums of '71 Taittinger Comtes de Champagne and
'45 Charles Heidsieck to start.

So, apart from having to repeatedly point out that Melbourne
wasn't Siberia, that there were no customs or passport formalities to
complicate life, that I hadn't had a frontal lobotomy and wouldn't
forget my 45 years in Sydney, that the fine dining opportunities
were greater in Melbourne, and that Australian was the language
of both cities, my main problem was moving my wine cellar from
Sydney to Melbourne. I had consolidated it in a self-storage area in
Pyrmont, the walls lined with ARC weldmesh and the centre filled

with Tooth beer crates, this providing single bottle access for all 15,000 or so bottles in the cellar.

While Clayton Utz had agreed to pay all my removal costs, I was loath to entrust my cellar to a commercial removalist, so I embarked on a plan to hire a trailer, and move it myself (with Suzanne's help, of course). I had a V8 Rover 3500 and hired a one-tonne trailer that we filled with almost one and a half tonnes of wine. (The remaining cellar was a further 21 tonnes.) To my dismay, even the most gentle of hills led to progressive loss of speed. Shortly put, it took us forever to complete the journey to Melbourne (and the similar self-storage facility I had set up there).

So a professional removalist company was hired, and the wine was packed in double thickness boxes. It was late spring by now, and the plan was to put it in containers on an overnight goods train to Melbourne. With the wine packed and ready to go, a train strike hit, with no certainty when it would be resolved. After much discussion, it was agreed the containers would be trucked to Melbourne, the only problem being that they were above permissible weight loads. If the trucks were weighed en route, they might well be stranded in hot weather.

Fingernails bitten to the quick, the wine arrived safe and sound, and was unloaded into the new cellar area, neatly packed in the centre of the room, leaving just enough room to walk around and place bottles in their allocated space in the ARC weldmesh covering all four walls. The dimensions of the room were different from those in Sydney, so it was impossible to precisely predetermine where the wines of each country (mainly French and Australian, but with significant German, Italian and Californian contributions plus wines from all other corners of the globe) would go, with varieties and styles from each country also ordered logically.

When I opened the first box (at random) I was puzzled: there were 12 different wines, with no rhyme or reason. Box two was the same, and almost immediately the awful truth struck home. I had arranged the wines in Pyrmont in vertical rows of 23 bottles each; the removalists had selected horizontally, walking around the room until the top layer was finished. A blackjack dealer in a casino could not have done a better job of shuffling the deck. Had I not planned to be there for five years, I would have given up; as it was, most of the job was done by Suzanne over a number of months.

I intended to partially overcome the financial hurdle of early, unfunded retirement by making wine from contract-grown grapes in rented space in someone else's winery (but using my winemaking equipment) in the 1985, '86, '87 and '88 vintages, but not selling any of the wine until I had retired and chosen a property for the ultimate establishment of a vineyard and winery.

And so it was that I made preparations for the 1985 vintage, entering into grape purchase agreements including one with my fellow law partner in Melbourne, Louis Bialkower, who had planted his Yarra Ridge vineyard in 1983, shortly after my arrival in Melbourne. The picking date was established: a Saturday, to allow friends and relatives to participate, but also to allow me to travel to Brisbane early on Sunday to participate in a 50-vintage tasting of Chateau d'Yquem with Comte Alexandre de Lur-Saluces (then a principal shareholder and chief executive of d'Yquem) in attendance.

At the last moment, and with virtually no notice, I had to fly to Los Angeles to represent the Australian subsidiary of Cadbury Schweppes UK in a three-way Australian, New Zealand and the parent UK company transaction. It was an important client, and I really had no choice. My stipulation was that I must return on Friday evening to allow me to get to Brisbane on the Sunday – I also

A Life in Wine

left behind a string of detailed instructions on the procedure for the first day of vintage.

Negotiations and document drafting proceeded more quickly than anticipated, and late on Thursday afternoon the English contingent suddenly started looking at their watches, and began to mumble about catching a plane back to London that night. I needed no encouragement: with the merchant banker from Australia also keen, we began to phone the airlines.

By having our tickets endorsed from Qantas to Continental, abandoning my clothes in the hotel laundry system (it was a walk-on, walk-off luggage trip), and proceeding direct from the business negotiation to the airport, we arrived 20 minutes before the plane was due to depart. First-class tickets helped, and we made it just as the doors were about to shut.

I arrived back in Melbourne very early on Saturday morning, with a grey sky and light drizzle. Without warning (mobile phones were a rarity then) I emerged from the gloom just as the picking team was agonising whether to pick or not. The rain had stopped, so I decided to pick. The taxi had passed by the house in South Yarra and allowed me to jettison my lawyer's suit for jeans, T-shirt and parka.

The grapes were loaded in 12-kilogram plastic crates onto a hired trailer with a nominal 1-tonne capacity – it was eventually filled with rather more than that. Late in the afternoon I headed off in my V8 Rover 3500 sedan, trailer in tow, with my six-year-old nephew Nick as co-pilot. We were headed for Baillieu Myer's Elgee Park winery on the Mornington Peninsula.

The grapes were protected by a tarpaulin, but the rain had returned, and I soon found the car (pushed by the trailer) had an alarming tendency to aquaplane as we approached red lights and stationary cars. Then the fuse for the windscreen wipers blew. With limited vision I made for an approaching service station. What I did not realise was that it was permanently closed, and that a piece of pipe protruding a few inches from the cement was about to puncture one of the tyres on the trailer.

Nick looked at me, and with a matter-of-fact voice said, 'You're lost, aren't you?' It may have been the least of my problems, but he was right. This was an inadequate protection against the homicide boiling in my veins until I saw a service station open for business on the other side of the street.

Several hours later we arrived at Elgee Park. The grapes were crushed into small dairy vat fermenters, and Suzanne drove us home to Millswyn Street in South Yarra. Since the previous Monday night, I had only been to bed twice, and I had to get up early the following morning to catch my flight to Brisbane. The all-day tasting was wonderful, sustained in my case by adrenalin flow dragged up from somewhere. I had to miss the dinner that night – and thus an 1899 brought by the Comte to accompany the '55, '45, '21 and 1900 (the oldest wine scheduled, and which was poured during the dinner with the three younger great wines, rather than in the last flight). Taking pity on me, I was able to taste each wine before I left for the plane, thence to South Yarra, and early on Monday morning back to Elgee Park to monitor fermentation.

The remainder of vintage passed without undue drama, thanks in no small measure to help from Dr Tony Jordan in making the chardonnay: I was more or less self-reliant with the red wines, but had far less expertise with whites. We had made small quantities of semillon and chardonnay at Brokenwood in 1982 which, if nothing else, convinced us that we needed someone with Iain Riggs' white winemaking experience.

Late in winter in 1985 I received a call from Jack Church of Warramate winery. I had let the Churches and Bailey Carrodus

ABOVE: *Coldstream Hills's first vintage – 1985. We solved the problem of transporting grapes to Elgee Park by renting a truck ...* BELOW: *... except some of the crates broke free after moving off from traffic lights.*

know that I was interested in keeping tabs on any property which came up for sale in Maddens Lane, Briarty Road or Hill Road, the three roads running up to or along the base of the Warramate Hills (also known as Steels Range). Jack told me an auction sign had gone up on an adjacent property, and gave me the name and phone number of the auctioneer.

More as a matter of curiosity that anything else I rang up the auctioneer to endeavour to find out what the reserve price might be. Needless to say, he wasn't about to name a precise figure, but – to my surprise – he said the price was likely to be around $250,000. Given that the land area was almost 40 acres (16 hectares), and the house substantial, I was – to put it mildly – intrigued, and I made an appointment to inspect the property with him that weekend.

I was still in negative net worth territory in the wake of the property settlement following my divorce (due to a legal decision which said the value of the law partnership had to be brought to account as a capital sum based on a price-earnings multiple, even though I had no access to that sum and, as a firm, we had taken goodwill out of the accounts).

Tony Jordan, Suzanne and I drove to the Yarra for the appointment from the Mornington Peninsula, where we had been monitoring the progress of the wines in barrel. It was a foul day, windy and wet, and when we arrived at the property next door to Warramate, there was no one to be found. We walked around for a while, discussing the property and the bargain it seemed to be, but were about to give up (we had arrived 15 minutes late) when Tony Jordan said 'I don't suppose it could be the property up the hill.'

This adjoined the upper boundary of the block we had been looking at, and had a house built like the bridge of a ship, a crescent on a suspended slab coming out the side of the hill. Suzanne, my children and her nephew Nick and niece Ali had often admired it, and speculated on the magnificent view it must have. My instinctive reaction was that it couldn't possibly be the property for sale, but it was a bare 100 metres to its front drive. There, in the entrance, was the For Sale by Auction sign.

A few minutes later we were standing in the house before a log fire, apologising as best we could for our lateness and confusion. Thirty minutes later we had agreed to buy the property, with a three-month settlement period, which the owners wanted to enable them to move to a new house by the sea at Lorne.

The price was $240,000, and on Monday morning I rang up my bank manager to explain that a cheque for $24,000 would be coming through the system later in the week, and – notwithstanding the absence of an overdraft facility – asked him not to bounce it, and that I was obtaining a mortgage from Partnership Pacific Limited to cover the purchase price. (Clayton Utz had its trust account with Westpac, and acted for Partnership Pacific. Academic considerations of conflict of interest seemed irrelevant.)

In fact I obtained a loan equal to 130 per cent of the purchase price, which provided the funds to also enable planting of the vineyard to begin in December 1985. The layout on the steep slopes of the amphitheatre was designed by Brian Croser, with input from David Paxton (noted McLaren Vale vigneron and viticultural consultant, still indirectly involved with Coldstream Hills's associated vineyards), who had been responsible for the establishment of Petaluma's vineyards in the Adelaide Hills on similarly steep slopes (one known affectionately as 'the widow-maker').

The idea of planting straight down steep slopes, as opposed to contour planting, was little known at the time. When, shortly after the amphitheatre had been planted, a field day was held on the vineyard, the Victorian Department of Agriculture was horrified, suggesting that the vines and all the topsoil would end up in the dam at the bottom of the hill. So too did Max Loader, a veteran viticulturist trained in Germany – of all places – and who we had briefly retained as consultant before agreeing to go our separate ways.

The planting (of pinot noir) was on the precipitous slope of what we called 'A Block', and, while challenging, was not as agonising as the planting of Brokenwood (or so I told myself). Conscripts from Clayton Utz had rallied to the cause, having been told in my written invitation that their future employment prospects would be greatly enhanced if they cared to join the planting team; many others also came along to variously lend moral or physical support.

Notwithstanding a 150mm downpour in December, only a few weeks after the completion of planting, the soil stayed where it was, long before protective grass cover had been established; the vines likewise. The soil is an ancient sandstone-derived mix of sandy clay loam and numerous fractured rock pieces, mountain soil which had been in place for countless millennia, and which wasn't going to move just because someone had put vines on it.

The house was barely 10 years old, but had internal design features which we felt had to be changed (apart from the curved shell of the house, which was fine): internal curves everywhere instead of corners; wire-cut bricks on feature walls which had to be bagged and painted; and an entirely new kitchen had to be installed (it had been the only room facing out to the Valley which didn't have floor to ceiling glass). By February 1986, the work had been completed, and we finally made the move from South Yarra, me to commute daily from Lilydale (by train) back to Melbourne.

In the meantime, we had bottled the chardonnay and pinot noir from the 1985 vintage. Because the quantity was small (120 dozen of each), and we wanted to use French burgundy bottles, Suzanne had become a dawn scavenger of the back door rubbish bins of Melbourne's leading restaurants, retrieving empty bottles which she then laboriously washed after removing the capsules and labels. They were stored in second-hand cartons in a large shed in the back garden, which was accessed by a small lane.

The day came for them to be taken to the winery for the bottling to take place. The majority had been moved to the open front verandah of the house; while Suzanne was loading the hired trailer with the remaining boxes in the back lane, those on the front verandah disappeared – in broad daylight, and in a matter of minutes. It turned out it was bottle collection day, and the council's bottle team was in peak form.

Frantic phone calls established the point where the bottles were to end up, and a high-speed car-plus-trailer chase resulted in Suzanne arriving first, and reclaiming her bottles. Discretion being the better part of valour, we did not try the collection route the following year.

We did, however, fight marauding rabbits and wallabies, first with orange-bag netting, and – in the face of defeat – by an electrified fence running through the hillside forest whence the vandals came. It worked well enough until wombats decided they would dig under and through the net, unperturbed by the electricity, making an auto route for the rabbits to pass through. Hammering steel droppers in the path of the holes worked for critical weeks, but it was not long before the wallabies worked out that a flying leap through the barbed wire strands at the top of the supposedly kangaroo-proof fence was not as life-threatening as might appear at first sight. (In fact, kangaroos have peacefully coexisted with the vineyard in increasing numbers, confining their attentions to the grass between the rows. It is

Boxing kangaroos in the Coldstream Hills vineyard.

the wallabies – and in recent years, deer – which devastate the young growing tips of the vines in spring and early summer.)

Suzanne and I also personally pruned the amphitheatre and house block chardonnay in the winters of 1986 and 1987. Young vines are easy and quick to prune, so we were able to tend the 5 hectares (12.5 acres) on our own, although it was a close call in 1987: as September approached, and then arrived, there were days when I was in the vineyard at first light for an hour's pruning before showering and changing into a suit for the train trip to Melbourne.

Vintage 1986 took place in the farm shed at Louis Bialkower's Yarra Ridge vineyard, to which I had moved my expanding collection of tanks, crusher and (in 1987) a 'new' Wilmes bag press (in fact, one of the first to have been imported into Australia, many years previously) to augment the basket press. In 1986 I had the assistance of New Zealand's Danny Schuster, then on a project to write a book on pinot noir which, despite several rewritings, was never published.

Brian Croser hosted the 17 May 1986 Single Bottle Club dinner at Bridgewater Mill with amazing food cooked by Cheong Liew, then of Neddy's, including pheasant and truffles cooked within a pig's maw for 1937 Yalumba/Caldwells Claret (ex the Hunter Valley), 1930 Yalumba Valley Claret (ex the Barossa Valley, for Len) and 1919 Yalumba Valley Claret (ex Eden Valley), all marvellous; and veal kidneys roasted in venison caul for the Burgundies (including '35 La Tache), and cheese for a bracket of seven Bordeauxs, including a magnum of '45 Chateau Ausone.

With our vineyard now named Coldstream Hills, we entered the Lilydale Wine Show (now the Yarra Valley Wine Show) in late October 1986, and I vividly remember catching a train from Melbourne to arrive for the exhibitors' tasting late in the afternoon, wondering on the way whether any of the wines had won medals. We had in fact won three trophies, the start of a string of successes. The following year we shared the trophy for Most Successful Victorian Exhibitor at the Royal Melbourne Show, winning it outright next year (1988). At the Victorian Wines Show the same year we won trophies for the Best White Wine and Best Red Wine of Show.

It was a pattern which continued in those early years. Jeremy Oliver had written in *The Age* on 14 April 1987, 'It is totally unfair that in his first commercial release, James Halliday should turn out such an unbelievable range of wines.' Paul de Burgh Day wrote, 'These wines really are monuments to the vintners' art, and I believe they will be seen as quintessential examples of their styles in the years

FOLLOWING PAGES: *Coldstream Hills labels featuring author's photography*

1986 *Coldstream Hills*

S E M I L L O N

H I L L C R E S T & S H A N T E L L E
V I N E Y A R D S

1991 *Coldstream Hills*

C H A R D O N N A Y

750ml LI   ALC. 13.0% VOL
BOTTLED BY COLDSTREAM WINEMAKERS LIMITED
LOT 6 MADDENS LANE, COLDSTREAM VICTORIA
VICTORIA PRODUCE OF AUSTRALIA

1992 *Coldstream Hills*

F U M E B L A N C

750ml LI   ALC. 12.5% VOL
BOTTLED BY COLDSTREAM WINEMAKERS LIMITED
LOT 6 MADDENS LANE, COLDSTREAM VICTORIA
VICTORIA PRODUCE OF AUSTRALIA

1992 *Coldstream Hills*

C H A R D O N N A Y

750ml LI   ALC. 13.0% VOL
BOTTLED BY COLDSTREAM WINEMAKERS LIMITED
LOT 6 MADDENS LANE, COLDSTREAM VICTORIA
VICTORIA PRODUCE OF AUSTRALIA

1997 *Coldstream Hills*

750 ml   C H A R D O N N A Y
13.5% alc./vol.
WHITE WINE PRODUCT OF AUSTRALIA · VIN BLANC PRODUIT D'AUSTRALIE

1993 *Coldstream Hills*

C H A R D O N N A Y

750ml LI   ALC. 13.5% VOL
BOTTLED BY COLDSTREAM WINEMAKERS LIMITED
LOT 6 MADDENS LANE, COLDSTREAM VICTORIA
VICTORIA PRODUCE OF AUSTRALIA

1 9 8 7 *Coldstream Hills*

N E W   P I N O T

Y A R R A   R I D G E   V I N E Y A R D

1 9 8 9 *Coldstream Hills*

C A B E R N E T
S A U V I G N O N

750ml   ALC.11.5% VOL
BOTTLED BY COLDSTREAM WINEMAKERS LIMITED
LOT 6 MADDENS LANE, COLDSTREAM VICTORIA
VICTORIA PRODUCE OF AUSTRALIA

1 9 9 0 *Coldstream Hills*

M E R L O T

750ml Ll   ALC. 13.0% VOL
BOTTLED BY COLDSTREAM WINEMAKERS LIMITED
LOT 6 MADDENS LANE, COLDSTREAM VICTORIA
VICTORIA PRODUCE OF AUSTRALIA

1 9 9 5 *Coldstream Hills*

P I N O T   N O I R

750ml Ll   ALC. 12.5% VOL
BOTTLED BY COLDSTREAM WINEMAKERS LIMITED
ST MADDENS LANE, COLDSTREAM VICTORIA
VICTORIA PRODUCE OF AUSTRALIA

1 9 9 5 *Coldstream Hills*

P I N O T   N O I R

750ml Ll   ALC. 12.5% VOL
BOTTLED BY COLDSTREAM AUSTRALASIA LIMITED
ST MADDENS LANE, COLDSTREAM VICTORIA
VICTORIA PRODUCE OF AUSTRALIA

1996 *Coldstream Hills*

750ML   P I N O T   N O I R

to come.' Finally, Huon Hooke (who has remained steadfast in his appreciation of Coldstream Hills wines over the years) wrote in the May/June 1987 *Epicurean* magazine that the 1986 Three Vineyards Chardonnay was 'pointing the future for Chardonnay in Australia – complexity rather than simple fruit coated with wood; harmony rather than obvious characters'.

Louis Bialkower had partially pacified his wife by promising that his involvement with Yarra Ridge would be limited to grape-growing, and that he would never allow the business to extend to winemaking (or so he told me). In a story which has been told hundreds of times since, the sight of grapes tended with the same love and attention as babies disappearing into someone else's wine was more than he (Louis) could bear.

Ironically, I had recognised the temptation (and, for me, the problem) from day one. Drawing on my observations and experience of the Californian wine industry, I had hit upon the idea of prominently crediting the grapegrower on the front label of the wine, in the hope that this would provide a sufficient sense of ownership and pride.

One of the most obvious Californian examples at the time was Heitz Martha's Vineyard Cabernet Sauvignon. Joe Heitz was the winemaker, and owner of the brand; Barney and Bella Rhodes owned Martha's Vineyard. The wine was the forerunner of the stratospherically priced icon wines of today, where ownership of vineyard and brand do in fact coalesce in an orgy of egomania. Back then, things were different, with Dick Arrowood's Chateau St Jean yet another to acknowledge the source of the grapes.

It is not the prerogative only of females to change their mind, and in 1987 Louis Bialkower changed his (and perhaps wife Vivienne's too). The net result was 1987 Coldstream Hills Yarra

Ridge Chardonnay, sold in a thoroughly confused market at the same time as 1987 Yarra Ridge Vineyard Chardonnay.

On the other side of the coin, as it were, I had verbally agreed to purchase Graeme Miller's pinot noir (from the then 10-year-old plantings) prior to his decision to sell Chateau Yarrinya to De Bortoli. Leanne De Bortoli and winemaker husband Steven Webber stood by that agreement, even though it was legally unenforceable and even though they would have far preferred to keep the grapes.

As far as I am concerned, it was a mark of the integrity which De Bortoli has displayed continuously since day one of the family's involvement in the Yarra Valley. There were more than a few who saw the move as a cynical opportunity to trade Riverina-sourced wine with the implicit claim of some Yarra Valley benediction. De Bortoli has never done this, clearly differentiating its Windy Peak range from its De Bortoli Yarra Valley, and (more recently) Gulf Station wines.

The 1987 Coldstream Hills Miller Vineyard Pinot Noir went on to come equal fourth in the 1988 Gault Millau Wine Olympics behind a 1985 Echézeaux of Henri Jayer, the highest placed wine from outside Burgundy in the 100 or so entries and, together with the 1988 Rising Shantell Pinot Noir of the following year, established Coldstream Hills Pinot Noir as one of Australia's best at that time. (In the first five years Coldstream Hills Pinots won 19 trophies, 40 gold medals, 28 silver and 13 bronze medals, a success rate of over 90 per cent.)

Even greater success came with the 1988 Coldstream Hills Rising and Shantell Vineyards Chardonnay in 1991. It came equal second (in a field of 200, including 80 from Burgundy) behind a 1986 Ramonet Le Montrachet; the judges commented, 'We don't

ELLE VOUS ATTEND DEPUIS 40 ANS

S I N G L E · B O T T L E · C L U B

4 · A U G U S T · 1 9 8 7

A R T   G A L L E R Y   O F   N S W

know where in the world this wine comes from. We know it's not French, but it ought to be.'

All the Sydney dinners up to 1987 had been held at Bulletin Place, but when John Beeston and Anders Ousbach hosted the 4 August 1987 dinner, we moved to the Art Gallery of New South Wales. A thoroughly eclectic array of (all French) wines were served in the presence of the French Ambassador, including '34 Bollinger ex magnum, '11 Moet et Chandon, three DRC Montrachets ('78, '76, '74, the '78 ranking as one of the greatest ever white burgundies), '57 Rayas Blanc, '45 Laville Haut Brion, '28 Vouvray (Bredif), a string of classic Bordeauxs, then 1897 Gruaud-Larose and 1874 Lafite, terminating in a run of Chateau d'Yquems, then 1893 Chateau Suduiraut (sublime) and the Club cognac, Louis XIII. In Michelin's language, worth the trip.

In the latter part of 1987 history repeated itself with a vengeance. Work had already begun on the construction of the Coldstream Hills winery at the top of the amphitheatre, and my partners now knew I really did intend to leave legal practice. The office had grown from six to 90 people, had moved twice, and was at least as profitable as Sydney: I had fulfilled my part of the bargain.

Then, out of the blue, as Suzanne and I (coming home from a dinner in Melbourne) turned the corner from Medhurst Road into Maddens Lane, an auction sign stared us in the face. This time there was no ambiguity: it was for the property adjacent to ours, which we had 'inspected' a little over two years earlier. While we did not know the owners very well, they owned the local farm produce store, and there had never been any gossip that they might be intending to sell. Indeed, Suzanne and I had from time to time discussed the 'what if' scenario of the property coming onto the market, and agreed that somehow we would have to try to find the funds to buy it – hopefully in some distant day.

I finally went to sleep that night resigned to my fate, and departed for my office the following morning in a depressed mood. A few hours after arriving Suzanne rang me to say, 'You've got to do something: Bailey Carrodus is walking over it; I can see him in the field glasses' (which she then and now keeps to ensure that things don't happen within our field of vision that she doesn't know about).

Forced to face up to the alternatives, I realised there were three choices: first, to postpone my retirement from the firm for up to 10 years and borrow the funds necessary to buy the property, plant it, and furnish the working capital until it started paying for itself. Second, to secure a number of financial partners happy to share the tax losses in the early years, a route suggested by my auditors and tax advisors (Peat Marwick, now KPMG). The third was to make a public issue of shares via the 'second board' listing procedure then available through the Australian Stock Exchange.

I opted for the third alternative, via the graces of Kleinwort Benson (technically KBA Management Services Limited) and David Fairfull, the merchant banker who had accompanied me (or I him) on that dash to Los Angeles two and a half years earlier. Armed with a letter confirming Kleinwort's willingness to underwrite an issue to raise $1 million, I once again exchanged contracts to purchase the property (for $270,000) within days of the For Sale sign going up. This was in early September 1987, a little before the stock market crash on Wall Street on 24 October 1987. As I stood in the shower each morning thereafter listening to the unfolding mayhem of the previous night's trading I was filled with foreboding. But the phone call to David Fairfull which always followed my arrival in the office was met with, 'Don't worry; it's only a small amount, and we'll get there, no problem.'

I did all the work on the prospectus myself; there was no solicitor for the underwriter; I arranged for the independent valuation reports; I entered into an exclusive worldwide distribution agreement with Negociants Australia; I handled all the Corporate Affairs Commission queries; and arranged for the printing of the prospectus. It was one of the fastest public issues in the history of the exchange, and was undoubtedly the cheapest. The issue opened on 3 December 1987, and closed on 4 January 1988, an 'impossible' time to raise funds.

It happened in part because of the modest size of the capital raising, which was itself limited by my desire to keep slightly over 50 per cent of the share capital, and offset by an employment contract which provided that I should not receive a salary or director's fee until the company was earning profits of $300,000 a year.

Had I possessed a crystal ball, and been able to look forward two years to early 1990, and to the two years which followed, there is no way I would have followed the same path. Whether I would have had the courage to defer my retirement and borrow the funds using my income stream is debatable, but in light of subsequent events, that might have been even more dangerous.

CHAPTER 11

COLDSTREAM HILLS
1988–96

Crystal balls being in short supply, and ever the optimist, I snuck away from Clayton Utz in April 1988 to the first vintage at our newly erected (or should I say, partly erected) winery. At the critical moment, the delivery of the final order for the unfired cement and straw bricks had been seriously delayed: it was in no way, shape or form the fault of our builder, Les Skate, who had carried out our home alterations for a derisory sum in 1985, and built our winery and its various extensions for the least imaginable price.

I had already appointed Kevin McCarthy as assistant wine-maker for the 1987 vintage at Yarra Ridge, and he came with me to Coldstream Hills in 1988, before moving on in the aftermath of the vintage to establish T'Gallant with wife Kathleen Quealy on the Mornington Peninsula. (T'Gallant was acquired by Beringer Blass

---

OPPOSITE: *Author with Saras, our female brown Burmese cat, a constant Coldstream Hills vineyard companion.*

in 2003.) In a pattern which became firmly established over the ensuing years, I departed for the London Wine Trade Fair in mid-May, my hands pitted, cracked and blackened by vintage, but then hastened back to look after the wines, and begin the slow process of racking the barrels.

On 23 September 1988 I hosted the dinner at Jacques Reymond's first Melbourne restaurant, coinciding year-wise with my 50th birthday. I sourced almost all the wines: ten from 1938, five from 1937 (the year of my conception), the remainder (bar one) from 1908, 1918 or 1928. The exception was '39 Chateau d'Yquem which, along with the '37, was provided by Brian Croser, who suggested they might be blended to make a '38.

By the simple expedient of only having three Bordeauxs from '38 (a dreadful year there) and focusing on '37 and '28 Champagnes, '38 Loire Valley white Burgundies and white Bordeauxs (very good in the Loire and Burgundy, fair to good for white Bordeaux), red Burgundies from '38 including Romanée St Vivant, a pair of '18 Sauternes and an '08 Cockburn Vintage Port to conclude, I escaped without criticism. Needless to say, Jacques Reymond's cooking was inspired.

Later that year Phil Dowell joined me from Domaine Chandon; I expected he would stay for two or three years, but in fact he stayed for 10 years before moving to Canada for Vincorp/Inniskillin, then Canada's largest wine group, with special responsibility for chardonnay and pinot noir. Once again, he surprised me by the length of his tenure there. He has a great sense of laconic, underplayed humour in classic Australian mode, emailing me at one stage to say that he, too, was going to write a book, entitled *Why I Hate Canadian Wine*.

Racking completed, bottling of the 1987 wines duly attended to, I turned my attention to planting the 30,000 vines on the newly

Each vine being planted in a hole made by an iron bar, Coldstream Hills, December 1985.

acquired property. The layout had been designed by Gary Crittenden (viticultural expert, director of Coldstream winemakers in the early years, and Mornington Peninsula eponymous winery owner) – he and Tony Jordan were two of the initial board of directors – and the all-important irrigation system had been handed to Chris Logan of Irrigation Supplies. From that point on, after the land had been prepared and the dams created, the endless post driving started, and I became chief overseer. The bulk of the labour came from the increasingly uncertain pool provided by the local Commonwealth Employment Services, notionally for the unemployed but in fact for the unemployable.

The 1985 amphitheatre plantings had been supervised by the energetic, entertaining but not always predictable Graeme Stevenson. Had it not been for my auto da fé at Brokenwood 15 years earlier, it is doubtful whether I would have been able to keep control, but I did. I was helped enormously by the moral encouragement (I only wish I could say it was the immoral encouragement) of the impossibly long-legged, strikingly beautiful, ash-blonde Olga Szymiczek, who these days runs Kangaroo Ridge Retreat, a bed and breakfast plus vineyard operation, with her partner.

There was a particularly hard patch in the centre of G Block chardonnay which the brawny, tattooed gentlemen of the CES studiously avoided. It was an old dam site which had been filled in not with clay, but with the clay subsoil of its banks. It was rock hard, and the usual spike and wriggle of the crowbar failed to produce the desired hole for the handful of Osmocote and the new vine's roots, followed by nice handfuls of topsoil to complete the interment. The special challenges of this block were left to me, and in silent fury I completed the planting. Most vines survived, but 15 years later they still showed up as a circular weak patch, looking to the unwary like the sign of the arrival of phylloxera.

The overwhelming problem for the planting of G Block (of over 8.7 hectares) was the non-arrival of the dripper line. Notwithstanding daily, and increasingly agitated, phone calls, we kept being held at bay by Netafim, the manufacturer. We had commenced planting reasonably early, and had the usual spring rainfall arrived, the problem would not have been so acute. It didn't, and it became increasingly obvious that the whole planting programme was in dire jeopardy.

In November I was judging at the National Wine Show in Canberra, and while absorbed in judging, torrential rain started beating down on the judging hall (which also served as the National tally centre during federal elections). For a split second, my heart and blood pulsed with elation – rain at last! – until I remembered I was 20 kilometres or so north of the vineyard.

A Life in Wine

I returned with adrenalin (not of the best kind) pumping through my veins, and absolutely not prepared to take no for an answer on the dripper line. If only my normally infinitely placid disposition had been stirred up two months earlier! Of the 20 kilometres (or some such number) required for the job, it transpired that all but ten had been completed long since, but the computer had refused to recognise the part order.

Murphy ruled supreme for that planting. The much more difficult amphitheatre area, on much steeper slopes and harder soil, had been 95 per cent successful. The strike rate on the G and Hill Block was abysmal, and, into the bargain, the pre-emergent herbicides had largely failed. By the time the water finally came on, we had a superb profusion of all the worst weeds, and a very indifferent display of vines. Even that first planting at Brokenwood, with no irrigation and rough blocks of clay, had been far more successful. So much for the viticultural Garden of Eden I had first seen and loved in 1979.

There was nothing for it. I got down on my knees, and vine by vine cleared the weeds by hand and gently tested each apparently dead rootling by lifting it imperceptibly. If I saw a growing root, which looked a bit like a bean shoot, I carefully eased the rootling back into the ground. If it showed some other signs of life, I planted another vine next to it, hoping one or the other would survive. If there was no sign of life at all, I removed the dead vine (occasionally horrified to see signs of life when it was too late) and planted a replacement one.

The last to be planted was the Hill Block, a separate mini-knoll that had lots of rock and even less topsoil than the rest. Having suffered months on my knees, moving tortoise-like from vine to vine, with knee callouses like those that barefooted sub-teenagers acquire from running everywhere without shoes, I was tempted to concede

ABOVE: *This gives some idea of the steep slope of the hill facing the pinot noir block in the amphitheatre at Coldstream Hills.*
BELOW: *All good wineries are built in the middle of vintage.*

ABOVE: *Early days of the top section of the amphitheatre. The north block has since been removed for winery buildings.*
BELOW: *A casual vintage lunch on the front verandah at Coldstream Hills. Suzanne's much-loved niece Ali is wearing the red top and blue bow.*

defeat. I didn't, though; while Hill Block (planted to pinot) developed more slowly initially, it caught up and occasionally produced better pinot than anything coming from G Block. A small extension of French clones 114 and 115 hasn't made much difference; the block still remains an enigma. But then that is the very essence of the most enigmatic of all grape varieties, pinot noir.

In 1989, as well as London Wine Trade Fair, I made the first of many trips to South Africa to participate in the selection of wines for South African Airways, which – naturally enough – flew me there for the judging. It was in the sanctions days, and the importance of gaining selection on the SAA wine list was massive. The judging was conducted in strict silence, the sheets handed to the SAA auditors, Peat Marwick, and at no time did you ever learn what wines you had judged; nor were you able to backtrack to find out what points you had given the wines which ultimately gained selection.

Peter Devereaux had asked me to join the panel, and during my stay I had dinner with Michael Fridjhon; this was the start of a long friendship. Not long thereafter, Devereaux died from a heart attack, and Michael Fridjhon took over as SAA's wine consultant. That first visit also came shortly after the election of President de Klerk; the progressive winemakers of the Cape (and others with the same political views) felt that de Klerk would wish to release Nelson Mandela and begin the dismantling of apartheid, but lacked the willpower and party support to do so.

History proved their pessimism unfounded, and South Africa slowly lost its pariah status. However, the paranoia which prevailed is still part of the national (white) psyche, and at none of the subsequent SAA tastings, nor the Diners Club competition (held each year for a given variety, with the prize going to the maker of the best wine), did I ever learn anything about the identity of the wines.

Other events organised by Michael Fridjhon, including the famous (or infamous) wine Test match between South Africa and Australia, the Dominion Wines benchmark tasting, and the Fairbairn Capital Trophy Wine Show, largely proceeded on the Australian model, with discussion on the wines allowed prior to their identity being revealed, and then full disclosure of the wines being made. The exception was the Test match, in which there was neither preference ranking nor discussion.

The South African Test match was modelled on two earlier challenges between California and Australia, both held in the latter part of the 1980s. The instigator of those was Len Evans, the sponsor Qantas. Each country selected 10 wines for each class (based on variety or blend), and the wines were ranked in order of preference (which eliminated differences in the use of points, or even the necessity of agreeing on which points scale should be used in the first place). Three judges came from each of Australia (Len Evans, Ian McKenzie and myself), California (Terry Robards, Andy Dias Blue and Daryl Corti) and three 'independents' from the UK (Oz Clarke, Robert Joseph and Anthony Rose).

The expectation (or hope) was that it should be an even contest, allowing both countries to feel satisfied. California had more to lose, because over 10 years earlier it had prevailed over France in a celebrated tasting organised by Stephen Spurrier. That had brought forth agonised calls of outrage and deception, because the judges (all French) did not know the identity of the wines being tasted! The second complaint was that the wines were too young. In a telling postscript, over a decade later a near-identical tasting (that is, most of the same wines of the original vintages) was staged. Once again, California came out a clear winner.

The first Qantas Cup was held at Rothbury Estate in the Hunter Valley, and was an embarrassingly lopsided affair, with Australia winning eight of the ten classes by considerable margins. The customary howls came from the losers: the wines had not had sufficient time to rest after coming from California, the wrong wines had been selected in the first place; the Australian judges hunted in a pack; and so on and so forth.

A return challenge was held in California in 1989. Robert Mondavi had offered to make his winery available at no cost as the location of the judging, and we were given the run of Cuvaison's guest house for the duration of the competition. This time the Californians had gone to an enormous amount of trouble in selecting their wines, with elimination tastings held as far afield as New York, with input from Peter Sichel.

Unfortunately, the result was the same: a win by a very large margin to Australia, which on both occasions had been very laidback about the selection process for its wines, and which arrived just in time for the competition. The Napa Valley vignerons must have scented the air, because some months prior to the tasting they passed a resolution that members of the Vignerons Association should have nothing to do with the event. Happily, both Mondavi and Cuvaison stood by their agreements to host us.

The second time around, the attack centred on the Australian judges, and on the fact that Rothbury, Seppelt and Coldstream Hills all had wines entered. (Coldstream Hills won the pinot noir class in both events.) The problem was that if you struck out the Australian judges' points, either on their individual wines or on the class as a whole, the result was largely unchanged – 'largely', because in some instances the margin between the Australian wines and the others was in fact increased.

It was clear that there was no hope of continuing the Qantas Cup in its bi-nation form. Instead, the Australian contingent set its sights on a New World–Old World competition, but before we got down to the hard business of deciding how the New World wines should be chosen, and finding a credible representative for the Old World (whose task would be even more difficult), Qantas made it clear that its sponsorship cup was empty.

Mind you, it could be argued that London's annual International Wine Challenge, staged in the run-up to the London Wine Trade Fair, and with 8000 or so entries, already told the Old World (and particularly France) everything it didn't want to know. While the numbers and results changed little from year to year, between the late 1980s and the end of the 1990s Australia had won twice the number of gold medals as France, but with half the number of entries: in other words, a four-to-one success rate. (Times have chanced since then: France has got its act together, and wins more gold medals than Australia, albeit with far more entries.)

When the South African Test match was held, the result was similar to that of the Qantas Cup. By chance, Coldstream Hills 1994 Reserve Pinot Noir tied for equal top wine of show, with an old (1953) fortified wine from the KWV. The howls of rage were similar, the accusations of bias likewise – notwithstanding that not only the judges but also the associates were involved in voting for the best wine of show. Once again, elimination of my preference ratings had no influence on the outcome.

The main complaint from the South African Old Guard was that the Test match was held 'too soon': 'We should have waited another five years.' Nothing could be further from the truth, as the event directly spurred a flood of South African vignerons to come to Australia to see what we were doing and whether the unthinkable was true: that we would actually tell them about winemaking practices and philosophies.

The 1988 Rising Shantell Chardonnay that did so well in the Gault Millau Competition won many trophies in Australia, including the special Chardonnay Trophy at the Canberra National Wine Show. Other conspicuous success came for the 1991 Pinot Noir, which won the George Mackey Trophy for the best wine exported from

Australia in the 12 months to October 1992, a feat equalled by the 1996 Reserve Chardonnay five years later. At that time Coldstream Hills was the only producer to have won the trophy twice, and this was an award which automatically cast its net over every wine exported in the relevant period. You did not choose to enter: every wine exported had to be tasted by an expert panel that met once or twice week in Adelaide, and outstanding wines were shortlisted, with a minimum amount (then 100 dozen) required to be exported. The 90 or so remaining wines were then judged in a special class at the Royal Adelaide Wine Show.

Woven through the turbulent years of 1989 and 1990 that were to follow came three exceptional dinners. The first two were in October and November 1989, the third in August 1990. The 18 November Single Bottle Club Dinner was at Tony Albert's house in Victoria Road, Bellevue Hill. A '79 Krug (magnum), '62 Veuve Clicquot La Grande Dame and '49 Louis Roederer Cristal preceded four '78 White Burgundies headed by Le Montrachet (DRC) served with truffle soup.

Tony's birth year was 1939, which was celebrated with '39 Yalumba Carte d'Or Riesling, flanked by '49 Chateau Chalon (from the Jura) and the amazing '23 Chassagne Montrachet of Vigneau. Then came '78, '72 and '42 La Tache, '39 Pommard Rugiens and '34 Gevrey Chambertin (both Barolet).

Five impeccable vintages of Chateau Latour ('62, '61, '59, '53 and '49) matched with poached beef fillet, while a selection of

THE 14th SINGLE BOTTLE CLUB DINNER

31st August, 1990 at Loggerheads

HOST: LEN EVANS,
on the occasion and the day of
HIS 60th BIRTHDAY

Savouries	Bollinger Annee Rare R.D. 1969 en Jeroboam Krug 1929
Broth with fungi	Duke of Wellington's Sherry 1850
Crayfish with oyster sauce	le Montrachet D.R.C. '86, '84 '82, '76, '69.
Marrow with bread & butter	Romanee Conti D.R.C. '87, '86, '85, '83, '81.
Lamb rissoles with gravy	Romanee Conti D.R.C. '78, '76, '74, '73, '72.
Pigeon with house vegetables	Romanee Conti D.R.C. '69, '67, '66, '64, '62.
Jindi Supreme	Romanee Conti D.R.C. '60, '52.
	Yalumba Barossa Valley Claret 1919.
	Victorian Ferruginous Fruity Burgundy c. 1890.
	Hunter Valley Dry Red 1855.
Steamed Pudding	Chateau d'Yquem '83, '76, '75, '70, '67, '22
Muscatels & Nuts	Tokay Aszu 5 Puttonos 1930.
	Yalumba Sir Douglas Mawson Expedition Port 1930.
	Rhinecastle G.I. Old Tawny 1930.
	Wynns Magill Vintage Port 1930.
	Club Cognac — Remy Martin Louis XIII

ABOVE: *A rather casual menu presentation for a fabulous Len Evans 60th birthday dinner (with commentary on p.176).*
FOLLOWING PAGES: *Coldstream Hills covered in the greatest snowfall in living memory.*

172

Australian cheeses were served with '47 Chateau Leoville Barton, '28 Chateau Langoa Barton, '21 Chateau Palmer and Chateau Cos d'Estournel, and 1874 Chateau Lafite.

Fruit and crème Anglaise came with '78 Chateau St Jean Late Harvest Riesling (Napa Valley), the famous (or infamous) '59 Kreuznacher Brüchs Trockenbeerenauslese (which I describe in the context of the Options Game, in Chapter 7) and '45 Chateau Latour Blanche. And so to birth-year '39 Seppelt Para Port, '39 Rhinecastle Old Dolcetto Port, '41 Tintara VSOP Pot Still Brandy and '49 Hine Grand Champagne Cognac.

As if to show that we were not the only ones to stage memorable wine dinners, the previous month (17 October 1989) I had attended a dinner staged by the de Burgh-Day Wine Company and Restaurant Quarter Sessions in Melbourne, which, for sheer class, was almost impossible to top.

At the time, there was enormous excitement about the quality of the '85 vintage in Burgundy, which had perfect weather from start to finish. Many of the wines in fact have developed more quickly than anticipated, and lack the intensity of a great vintage. But, as so often is the case, the DRC has proved an exception. On the other hand, '78 is one of the all-time great vintages in Burgundy, as good or better than '45, '49 and '59. (We really have to wait and see about the vintages of 1999, 2005 and 2009.)

So the dinner: '82 Krug to commence; from then until the penultimate wine, it was all DRC: '78 and '70 Montrachet, followed by '85 Echézeaux, Grands Echézeaux, Romanée St Vivant, La Tâche and Romanée-Conti. Next came the incomparable '78s: Echézeaux, Romanée St Vivant, Richebourg and Romanée-Conti.

Richebourg (DRC) of '64 and '37 Richebourg (Leroy, co-owner of DRC) came at the end, with a probably superfluous '40 Grande

Champagne Cognac shipped by Berry Bros and Rudd. Sheer perfection from start to finish, the matching dishes immaculate. (I have to confess that, seeing the profligacy with which the '78s were being served, I managed to secure an open bottle of the Montrachet and Romanée-Conti, stored under the table by the leg of my chair, and drank each of them.)

Impossible to top? No, as the Single Bottle Club dinner of 31 August 1990 to celebrate Len Evans' 60th birthday proved. Caviar blinis accompanied '69 Bollinger Année Rare RD in Jeroboam and the famous '29 Krug. The Duke of Wellington 1850 Sherry completed the introductory formalities, and then it was into the serious business of the DRC: Le Montrachet '86, '84, '82, '76 and '69. Then came 17 vintages of the world's greatest wine, Romanée-Conti: '87, '86, '85, '83, '81, '78, '76, '74, '73, '72, '69, '67, '66, '64, '62, '60 and '52.

The last two Romanée-Contis came with '19 Yalumba Barossa Valley Claret, circa 1890 Victorian 'Ferruginous Fruity Burgundy' (Mora Mora Wines) (which had clearly been lightly fortified, tasting more like a wonderfully sweet and voluptuous tawny port) and 1855 Hunter Valley Dry Red, in a beautiful dark green glass bottle. It, too, showed signs of an incomplete fermentation or fortification. Huge and intense, it had a mix of aldehyde and volatility in its bouquet, but was still drinkable and quite fascinating.

Six vintages of Chateau d'Yquem followed: '83, '76, '75, '70, '67 and '22, then to celebrate the birthday, '30 Tokaji Aszu 5 puttonyos, '30 Yalumba Sir Douglas Mawson Expedition Port, '30 Rhinecastle G.I. Old Tawny and Wynns Magill Vintage Port. The Club cognac, Louis XIII, marked the close. If you were to even attempt to reassemble those wines today in Australia, a war chest of anything less than $250,000 would leave you short of the mark.

S uccess in wine competitions was one thing, great wine dinners another, but by the end of 1989 Australia was plunged into 'the recession it had to have', as Treasurer Paul Keating so daintily phrased it. Not long thereafter the world followed suit, although almost nowhere was the downturn as deep or as long as it was in Australia. In turn, the market for super-premium wines shrank dramatically: sales over $20 per bottle continued only for icon or boutique producers. Most prices between $20 and $30 were pulled under $20, sometimes well under.

The most celebrated example was the Lindeman Coonawarra trio of Limestone Ridge, St George and Pyrus. With a theoretical price in the low $30 range, but an actual price in the high $20s, Lindemans reduced the price so that at $19.95 there was some margin for the retailers in what was expected to be a sales bonanza. The retailers couldn't resist the temptation, and engaged in a 'I'll match the lowest price' campaign, which resulted in the wines selling for $14.99, less than half the price of a month previously.

Coldstream Hills, as a result of the upheavals in wine prices, moved relatively early, reducing the price of the Reserves from the mid $20s to under $20, and the varietal wines from just under $20 to under $15. It was an exceedingly painful exercise, for I took the view that I had to retrospectively compensate our distributor, Tucker Seabrook, for all the stock they still had on their books, and, through them, all the retailers and restaurants for the stock they still had at the old prices. To do otherwise would have penalised those who had supported us all along, and given the newcomers who joined the party (and there were many) an unfair price advantage.

Sales took off and never looked back, but the impact on the profit and loss account was disastrous. We raised capital through a placement and a rights issue which saw Hugh Johnson become a significant shareholder and a director. It was the action of a true friend, and I shall be eternally grateful for it.

Clawing back the gross margin was nigh on impossible in the short run, and like so many companies at the time, the National Australia Bank (NAB) made my life a misery. (I had changed from Westpac following a visit by the account manager, whom I had not previously met. He declined wine, tea, coffee or beer, opting instead for a cup of hot water. Not long thereafter I received a letter on bank letterhead written by the manager telling me he was about to fulfil his lifelong ambition to become a Baptist Minister in the Solomon Islands. I had every intention of framing the letter, but it was accidentally thrown out.) But I was to learn the change would prove to be a case of jumping from the frying pan into the fire.

The flames were fanned by a piece of research put out by investment bank Dominguez Barry. It said that of the 400 wineries in Australia in 1990, only a handful were profitable, and that by the end of the decade there would be fewer than 200. In fact there were well over 1000 at the end of the decade, and from a starting point of 500+, not 400. The report completely missed the point about the financial motives of the majority of the winery owners, and failed to understand the implications of the export boom which was by then well and truly underway.

Nonetheless, it caused the trading banks to embark on a course of 'reducing their exposure' to the industry. Coldstream Hills had its working capital requirements funded by bank bills with interest rates around 20 per cent. It had never defaulted on a payment due to the bank nor breached any loan condition. Nonetheless, the bill finance was 'at the bank's pleasure', and less than a week before the bills fell due for rollover, the manager of Coldstream Hills' account informed me that a decision had been taken to call them in. When I pointed out the implications, and asked whether the bank really wished to become involved in the running of a winery, he answered no, saying that the decision had been taken higher up.

After much discussion, he reluctantly gave me the name of the bank officer who had made the decision. I requested an appointment to see him, but after a 48-hour delay, I was told the person in question (whom I am sorely tempted to name) had refused to see me or discuss the decision: it was final. Obviously I was at my wits' end, with oblivion staring me in the face.

Then something stirred in my memory. Back in the middle 1970s, while I was an Assistant General Manager at

Commercial Continental Limited, I had a man seconded from the Commercial Banking Company of Sydney working for me in loans recovery and administration. He was unhappy that he did not have an official title to put on correspondence, and I gave him one (loans administration manager) on the spot when he raised the issue with me in the pub one Friday afternoon. He was inordinately grateful for such a small thing, and I thought no more about it.

He returned to mainstream banking, and over the next 15 or so years had risen steadily through the bank's hierarchy (the NAB had taken over the Commercial Banking Company of Sydney in the meantime) and was now in Melbourne in a very senior position indeed. I rang him, and within 24 hours the decision had been reversed. It was not so long thereafter that David Fairfull once again came to my aid by introducing an English group wishing to make a substantial investment in Australia, and interested in Coldstream Hills (or Coldstream Winemakers Limited, as it then was).

They made no secret of the fact that they wished to ultimately diversify the company's activities and (by virtue of my long experience in corporate law) I was under no illusion that they might well use the 30 per cent shareholding they in due course obtained to achieve outcomes I opposed. But the economy as a whole, and the wine industry in particular, was still doing things tough, and the NAB episode had been thoroughly unsettling.

Indeed, I had been involved in discussions with

Petaluma Limited, exploring possibilities of some kind of merger (with Coldstream Hills the minor partner, of course), but Brian Croser's board prevented the discussions going past first base. So the placement was done with shareholder approval, and the English investors came on board, headed by Garnett Harrison. At my suggestion, Hugh Johnson departed, because it seemed likely that there would be major changes ahead – parking stations in Hong Kong was one proposal for the use of the surplus funds the company now had.

In fact, a number of things happened. The mid-rank managers at the NAB fawned all over me, offering this, that and the other thing – offers I had pleasure in rejecting. Next, as 1992 passed, the industry started to gain ground on the domestic market, and (after a hiccup in 1989) exports were continuing to grow rapidly. Third, and most unexpectedly, the English investors fell in love with the industry as a whole, and Coldstream Hills in particular.

The business grew, first with the outright acquisition of the partially planted Briarston vineyard in late 1993, and then with the syndicated development in 1994 and 1995 of two large Upper Yarra vineyards, Deer Farm and Gladysdale. Growth in production was still constrained by a continuing grape shortage in the Yarra Valley, and by small crops in 1994 and 1996, but we were gradually recovering margins and starting to see the first benefits of economy of scale.

Over this period, Single Bottle Club Dinners had been oases of relief and pleasure. Proceedings got underway at the 11 September 1991 dinner with two magnums of champagne: 1933 Hautvillers (completely oxidised) and 1893 Bollinger (magnificent, gas still evident on the tongue, the honeyed peachy fruit with not a hint of decay).

Pot au Feu de Langoustine was matched with five Montrachets: 1983, '76 and '69 from the Domaine de la Romanée-Conti, and '83 and '78 from Remoissenet and Colomb Marechal respectively. The sulphur dioxide-dominated '78 was a major disappointment, but the three DRCs lived up to their exalted reputations, led by the youngest and the oldest, and the Remoissenet also had that almost unctuous, layered richness that only (Le) Montrachet achieves.

Then followed 13 of the greatest 20th century vintages of Chateau Latour: '70, '66, '62, '61, '59, '55, '53, '49, '48, '45, '37, '29 and '21. Cork killed the '53 and '45 and compromised the '61 and '21; the '70 was too young; the '37 as tannic and brawny as expected (the '30s was a wretched decade); and the '62, despite being a magnum, was outclassed.

At the other end of the spectrum, the '29 was a magnificent bottle of a magnificent wine, laden with unctuously rich and sweet cassis fruit, almost into essence, yet not jammy nor porty. The '49 was another great bottle, not far behind the '29, and a hair's breadth in front of the '59.

Then came six vintages of Chateau d'Yquem: '76, '75, '70, '45, '19 and '12, the '76 and '70 without fault but comprehensively outclassed by the other four. Even then, the '75 proclaimed its class and continues to grow in bottle, with no end in sight, and we were dead lucky with the '19 and '12 bottles, both outstanding.

It was left to the deservedly legendary '45 to challenge the '29 Latour, and come out with the same points (19.5/20). My rhapsodic tasting note ended 'ultimate Marilyn Monroe'. Cockburn's 1963 Vintage Port and 1893 Delamain Grande Fine Cognac were not really needed, but did bring a great dinner to a successful conclusion.

It might seem hard to challenge that dinner, but Ian Macnee wasn't daunted when he hosted the dinner held at Loggerheads on 10 September 1993. There was a string of great wines, but the highlight was the 1865 Chateau Kirwan, the third bottle I had tasted (or provided) of this stupendous wine. It had the colour and the potency of a great 20-year-old Bordeaux at the start of its life. Except for the fact that I had drunk two bottles of the wine in London in 1981 (well before Hardy Rodenstock had started 'discovering' the Thomas Jefferson 1787 Chateau Lafite and other Jefferson wines, including d'Yquem), I and the others at the dinner might have wondered whether it could possibly be 128 years old.

But I had purchased and drunk two bottles of the Kirwan at London restaurant Au Jardin des Gourmets in Greek Street, Soho, (having read Michael Broadbent's ecstatic tasting note in the first edition of his *Great Vintage Wine Book*) and been transfixed by their youth, vigour and sheer quality. (I was not to know it in 1993, but in 2001 I was to share an even greater wine from the same vintage – more of which anon.) Those Au Jardin bottles were slightly different, one showing a touch of wet cork, the other perfect – as was the bottle at Loggerheads.

Len Evans hosted the 19th dinner, on 15 September 1995, to celebrate his 65th birthday. The theme was 1930 (birth year), 1929 (year of conception) and then a series of old to very old wines that were rare and unusual. Serge Dansereau was chef, and excelled himself.

Oscietra Caviar on salmon sushi accompanied three wonderful bottles of champagne, still full of life and vigour: '29 Pommery & Greno, '29 Bollinger (the best) and '11 Perrier Jouet. We were equally lucky with the trio of ancient German rieslings – '29 Forster Kirchenstuck, '21 Niersteiner and 1887 Marcobrunner. The '21 Niersteiner was a vibrantly luscious wine of beerenauslese sweetness balanced by acidity, and the 1887 Marcobrunner was past its best, but eminently drinkable.

Len remained a Bordeaux man to the end of his life, however great his love for Domaine de la Romanée-Conti. So three flights of Bordeaux followed, mainly focused on the great twin vintages of 1929 and '28. A pair of '30 Yalumba Claret (impossibly volatile) and 1865 Chateau Laroque (St Emilion), ethereal and frail, a grandmother still with a smile on her face, were the final reds.

The two sauternes, '17 Chateau d'Yquem and 1770 Sauternes, were the high point of the dinner, both 20/20 as far as I was concerned (and I think the others). Michael Broadbent had clearly not tasted the '17 d'Yquem, and gives short shrift to the vintage. This was a great old bottle of a great wine (d'Yquem made multiple bottlings in those days, basically on demand). Luscious cumquat and mandarin fruit were balanced by perfect acidity stretching out the lingering finish.

But it was the 1770, procured by Anders Ousbach in England, in a virtually clear, hand-blown bottle in a shape I have never seen before or since, that inevitably stole the show. A bouquet of candy, mint and camphor led into a palate of incredible intensity, with Callard & Bowser butterscotch flavours offset by immaculate acidity; it grew and grew in the glass. Obviously pre-dating paper labels, and being generic sauternes at the dawn of the style (it was sold to Anders by a highly reputable retailer as 1770 to 1780), its exact provenance was unknown, but irrelevant.

The final trio were an anti-climax, although the 1834 Roriz, like the sauternes, made in the early years of vintage port, was fault-free, simply aged into tawny, rather than vintage, port style.

In 1995 BRL Hardy made an indirect and tentative approach to acquire Coldstream Hills that, in terms of my personal involvement, I firmly rejected. Discussions with Petaluma began again, this time in a very different atmosphere. The deal hammered out would have given the English investors in Coldstream Hills a handsome return on their investment (particularly once exchange rate movements were taken into account), with the option of remaining shareholders in an enlarged company if they so wished, and would have left Coldstream Hills as a listed company, majority owned by Petaluma, but with a much larger Victorian business base. (The plan envisioned Mitchelton and Taltarni becoming subsidiaries, with my role of managing director covering all three companies.)

Shareholder approval from both companies would have been necessary, but the independent valuations needed had been completed and the loose ends tidied up. I shook hands with Brian Croser in the Adelaide Hills, and the deal was as good as done.

Except for one thing. As I sat in my office one Saturday morning in May 1996, about to depart the following day for the London Wine Trade Fair, the telephone rang. It was Southcorp Group Chief Executive Graeme Kraehe, ringing me to tell me that on Monday morning Southcorp would be announcing a takeover offer for Coldstream Australasia Limited (as the public company was by then known) at 96 cents per share. It was followed by a further

FOLLOWING PAGES: *Early morning mists, common in autumn, provide a constant fairyland, visible from verandah of author's house.*

courtesy call from Bruce Kemp, chief executive of the Southcorp Wine Group, whom I knew well, and liked.

Plane flights cancelled, and emergency board meetings convened, it was decided to retain BT Australia as advisors to the company. Quite early in the piece it emerged that merchant bank A had approached merchant bank B, and suggested that if a takeover offer were made at around 96 cents, it was likely to be successful. Merchant bank B then went to Southcorp, which duly made the bid. The less said about the circumstances the better, other than to make it clear that Southcorp was in no way involved in any doubtful activity.

Moreover, from day one, I took the personal position – as an employee (without a service contract) and shareholder – that if there was to be a takeover offer, and Petaluma didn't wish to become involved in a bidding war (which, given the size of the two companies, it didn't), then Southcorp was the only company with which I was prepared to do business. I knew all the senior winemaking team very well, and liked them all, but Bruce Kemp was also a key player as far as I was concerned.

In light of the financial success of BRL Hardy, and the utter fiasco of the Southcorp-Rosemount merger, the collapse of the Southcorp business, the loss of almost all its key executives in the bloodbath which followed the merger, and the collapse of the share price of Southcorp, which rendered it hugely vulnerable to takeover, this seemed, over the next five years, a very bad decision.

Nonetheless, it was one I was fully entitled to make. My duty as a director was to obtain the best price I could for the company's shareholders, but that duty did not extend to making myself a sacrificial lamb. Since it was obvious that any alternative bidder would seek some indication of my intentions, Southcorp was effectively without competition, and all I could do was negotiate on price. Even here, the English investors played a strange role, and in the outcome the offer price was increased by only ten cents, to $1.06 per share.

The question no one will ever know the answer to was whether Southcorp would have crossed the 50 per cent barrier if I had held firm and refused to sell. Unless it reached 50 per cent, the bid would have failed altogether, which would have been the best result. The worst would have been a company majority owned by Southcorp, but with large minority shareholdings, including that of me and my family.

With a longer perspective (particularly the unforeseeable events that were to unfold in 2010), I have no regrets about my decision to accept the offer. Later in 1996 Southcorp acquired the Margaret River winery Devil's Lair, a logical extension of its desire to invest in regional wineries. In the upshot, I was appointed group winemaker for Devil's Lair, Coldstream Hills and the Hunter Valley trio of Lindemans, Hungerford Hill and Tulloch.

The latter three had all played a significant role in my early moves into wine, none more so than Lindemans. If I had said to my father in the 1960s or '70s, 'Dad, one day I will become group winemaker for Lindemans', he would have known I was under the influence of some hallucinogenic drug. His reaction would have been much the same even if I had said it in 1988, on the eve of my departure from law, or shortly prior to his death in December 1990.

When I left Sydney to move to Melbourne after the 1983 vintage, I was delighted that I would no longer have to worry about the utterly unpredictable nature of the Hunter's summer climate: 40°C one day, pouring 50mm or more of rain the next day.

It was thus with the ultimate déjà vu feeling that I made my first trip back to the Hunter as group winemaker, looking apprehensively at towering cumulo-nimbus clouds gathering on the horizon. This apprehension mirrored my broader concerns about the mindset of the South Australian base of Southcorp, firmly anchored by Penfolds, Wynns and Seppelt.

I knew from a decade of marketing Coldstream Hills' wines within Australia that it was a waste of time trying to persuade the blue or lesser bloods of Adelaide that they should take any wine made outside South Australia seriously. Perth and Brisbane were far more receptive markets.

Even more telling was the disdain for Hunter semillon, a variety used as a workhorse in the Barossa Valley with a bridle of low-quality oak. Nonetheless, I was determined to arrest the downward spiral of Lindemans' two Hunter Valley wines: semillon and shiraz. Critical to this plan was my 'persuading' (by a mixture of verbal carrot and stick) Coldstream Hills assistant winemaker Greg Jarratt that he should take up the role of executive winemaker for Lindemans.

With considerable reluctance, he agreed to go in December 1997, and I set about learning as much as I could about contemporary winemaking practices with Hunter semillon, and tasting the wines against a precise background of technique and chemical composition. We agreed on a plan for the 1998 vintage, and the wine was made and bottled well before the Hunter Valley Wine Show later that year.

The wine won a trophy for Best Current Vintage Semillon, and we sat back waiting for the waves of congratulations. Instead, there was silence, most profound from the sales and marketing department. I was defeated, but in an ironic twist, Greg was not. Having initially hated the Hunter, its often appalling weather, and his enforced separation from pinot noir and chardonnay, he fell in love. In love with the region, his fellow winemakers, and Jules (Julie) his partner, who

A Life in Wine

Attending a Rugby Union Bledisloe test match in Auckland,
New Zealand: happy before the match, but not after. From L to R:
Ken Gargett, Nick Stock, Nick Ryan, Stuart Gregor and author.

accompanied him back to the Yarra when he returned in October 2001. (Greg Jarratt continues as winemaker at Coldstream Hills, with partner Jules and newly arrived son Charlie.)

To use Bruce Tyrrell's words (circa 2009), Hunter Valley semi-llon has entered a golden age. The advent of screwcap has meant winemakers can hold back part of their production for five or more years prior to release free of the fear that 30 per cent or more would be destroyed by the twin problems of cork taint and sporadic (random) oxidation.

This has in turn meant an increase in the number of single-vineyard wines – Tyrrell's has half a dozen, Brokenwood and others two or three – released when mature. Lindemans, the colossus of Hunter semillon through to 1970, is now a minor player at best.

CHAPTER 12

WINE TASTINGS OVER THE DECADES

Looking back at the 1960s and 1970s, I feel I was swept up in a series of seemingly disconnected events that ultimately formed a pattern. At the time I did not see any of those events as part of a bigger picture. In the '70s I began writing columns on imported wines for the now long-defunct *Wine & Spirit Buying Guide*, in some instances quite literally learning on the job. Thus on one occasion, with a deadline looming, I drove across from my flat in the eastern suburbs of Sydney to the lower north shore, where the *Guide* had its office.

The subject was Asti Spumantes, and the tasting started at 7am, because I was due in my law office for a 9.30am conference. I recall the event with the utmost clarity 35 years later purely because of my disdain for the spumante style.

OPPOSITE: *The serious business of savouring the bouquet.*

Another tasting took place on an Easter Monday morning on the cold cement floor of Brokenwood's winery. Arranged in rows were the 4-litre wine casks that then accounted for over 65 per cent of total domestic wine sales. Most were white burgundy, riesling (meaning anything but true riesling), claret and burgundy. Their varietal composition was not specified, and was in any event irrelevant.

Crouching on the cement floor to write tasting notes was bad enough. Even worse was the knowledge that there was no batch number, let alone use-by date, so what I tasted and what my readers tasted could be very different. I was also realistic enough to know that only a small percentage of those who purchased wine casks would dream of reading tasting notes. Shelf-talkers with points (the small cards retailers display next to wines that show the wine's tasting notes and, more importantly, points: 'James Halliday 80 points', for instance) might be the only avenue.

As I have recounted, we made our first two Brokenwood wines in 1973, and I entered another disconnected world, tasting red wine before its vinous umbilical cord was severed by pressing the must (the skins) and seeing the blood-red fermenting juice go to barrel to complete its fermentation, then tasting it again and again in the weeks and months that followed. This, too, was strictly learning on the job.

There was no predetermined chronology in these events, but they had something in common: accepting the wines for what they were, and simply seeking to evaluate their quality. By a process not far removed from osmosis, I had begun to create an unspoken, inner language or framework that allowed me to see whether or not a wine had balance and length, the two cornerstones of quality. I did not realise it then, but this was the training ground for my ultimate initiation into wine show judging.

Yet even before we had planted the first vines at Brokenwood, I had embarked on an entirely different odyssey, learning about the great wines of France (and, to a lesser degree, Germany). I read all the books I could find, memorising all the classed growths (or Chateaux) of Bordeaux, and remembering whether they were first, second, third, fourth or fifth growths – and from which communes they came.

I likewise learnt as much as I could about the even more complex tapestry of Burgundy, with its Grand Crus, Premier Crus and Village wines, and the profusion of winemakers who had even tiny holdings (a tenth of an acre or less) in those crus. There were only 61 makers of classed growth Bordeaux, but hundreds upon hundreds of makers of Burgundy. (It's true that across the Gironde in Bordeaux, St Emilion had 565 classified wineries in two tiers and Pomerol had over 100, but no official classification.)

The potential for getting lost in the bureaucratic nightmare of Germany was another thing again. It was compounded by changes in the system that only Lewis Carroll could suggest made things easier; the unintelligible gothic printing of the labels was the nail in the coffin.

But this was just background knowledge to our tutored wine tastings every Monday at Len Evans's Bulletin Place. I cannot remember how many months went by while we still had our training wheels on, tasting and discussing great wines with the bottles in front of us. But we soon embarked on a completely different type of wine assessment, the vehicle being the Options Game that I have described in Chapter 7.

You had to think about the wine's regional origin, its status within that region, and its age. (I became known as the vintage palate because I had more success with this subject than the others did.)

On the assumption that it was a French red wine, region became co-extensive with variety: pinot noir for Burgundy, cabernet sauvignon and/or merlot for Bordeaux, and shiraz (with or without viognier) for the Northern Rhône Valley.

At the heart of this was the complex matrix between vintage (good or not), age (young or old), style (especially relevant in Burgundy) and quality. Thus you hoped to guess the wine's maker or exact origin before the first options question was asked; then would come a pulse of hope where that question accorded with your hunch, or momentary dejection where it was something quite different. (You remained in the game for all five questions.)

Before I left for Melbourne in 1983, perforce abandoning my Monday trysts, my taste buds had been honed to a fine edge by the constant practice, and Len Evans and I contested top spot. (A cumulative monthly score was kept, and periodically a new 'world series' would be declared.)

The move also happened to come at a time when I was becoming more heavily engaged in wine show judging (since my initiation in 1977). Thus not only did I stop the options practice schedule, but I also became focused on the polar opposite: no thought about who might have made the wine, just a single-minded consideration of its quality. Since you already knew the variety and most likely the vintage, the differences between the best wines were wafer thin.

Throughout the 1980s and much of the 1990s, it was accepted that 180 wines per day per judge was a reasonable number, starting at 8.30am and finishing at no fixed time: you kept going until the day's work was done, hopefully by no later than 5pm. Moreover, the size of some of the classes – notably chardonnay and shiraz – grew remorselessly. It became common (by way of example) to be confronted with over 100 chardonnays, all of the same vintage. This

ABOVE AND BELOW: *The never-ending tastings for the annual Wine Companion, staged in the loft of one of the Coldstream Hills winery buildings.*

was a far more demanding challenge than judging (say) 50 chardon-nays, then 50 shirazs. But until the numbers reached 150 or more in a given class, you had no option but to doggedly work your way through the wines.

The long table at which you worked was divided into a chess-board-like pattern, with numbered squares that corresponded to the numbers on the judging sheets. For many years I would observe the colour, and smell the bouquet, very carefully, making notes of what I found. When I had become accustomed to the rigours of show judging, I found that 90 per cent of the total information I would accumulate for 90 per cent of the wines came from the bouquet.

I would proceed to smell every wine in the class before tasting any, and would move each glass forward (good) or backwards (bad). But each move could be as small as a millimetre, and Len Evans (for so long Chairman of the Sydney Wine Show) quickly became aware of my silent fury if he picked up a glass and did not return it to its precise spot. (Especially bad wines would result in the acronym DNPIM on my score sheet, standing for 'do not put in mouth'.)

Thus the second round – actually tasting the wine, writing a few more notes, and only then ascribing a score – was far quicker. But even then it would be necessary for me to take my six or so top wines, move them to the front of the table, and go backwards and forwards to find which I considered the best (possibly to sim-ply confirm my earlier evaluation), see whether the next best was clearly superior to the other four wines, and which of those were truly of gold medal standard (18.5 points out of 20). Thus the top gold might receive 19.5 (a rare score), the second wine 19 points, the other(s) 18.5 points.

As the years went by, I would combine the smell and taste steps, and forthwith give points to all the wines I considered worthy of a silver medal (17 to 18 points), bronze medal (15.5 to 16.5 points) or no award – but even here I would use anything between 12 points (seriously faulty) through to 15 points (no fault, of sound commercial quality, but lacking intensity and/or varietal character).

One of the unique features of Australian and New Zealand wine shows (and some other New World shows, but never European shows) was that at the conclusion of each class all three judges (and the associate judges) would call out their points in turn, the panel chair collating them and leading the discussion on the best wines or those where there was some discrepancy in the points. Every judge must be able to explain precisely why they gave their points, which in this context meant that they were out of step in terms of liking or disliking a wine more than their counterparts. (Because I had a second journalistic use for my score sheets, my written comments were usually much longer than those of others on the panel.)

This discussion was most valuable when it turned on questions of style, not simply quality. Was the wine an example of where the industry had come from (buttery, peaches and cream, oaky chardonnay) or where it was headed to (finer, more elegant and subtle chardonnay)? Of course there were likely to be examples of both styles, and it still remained necessary to consider just how well the wine had been handled in the winery.

I also judged in many overseas wine shows, in Europe usually according to INAO (the French appellation authority) protocols: one wine at a time, score sheet immediately handed in, and no discussion. A fast and easy way to judge wines, computer-calculated, but needing some sophisticated programmes to give statistically relevant outcomes.

By the latter part of the 1990s I had become Chairman of Judges (on a three- to four-year term) at various capital city and numerous regional shows. Particularly at capital city shows this involved discussion with the committees on various procedural matters (for example, should there be some new classes, and some deleted?); the choice of judges, most particularly the international judge or judges (initially limited to the Canberra National Wine Show, but spreading to most shows over the years); and the question of glassware. It was also the Chair's job to distribute the classes to be judged each day between the three, four or five panels. This involved a spread of varietal classes over the three or four days of judging so that no one panel received a mono-diet of one variety, and ensuring that each panel had the same number of wines to judge each day. A further task was to move the two judges other than the panel chair so that each judge ended up on a different panel each day, with a new panel chair and a new peer judge. A computer programme would have been handy, but it was all done manually.

It so happened that I was instrumental in the move away from small but heavy glasses made in China in an ISO standard shape and size to much larger Riedel glasses (Ouverture magnum). At the time I was Chair of both the National and the Sydney shows, the former notable for its willingness to accept recommendations.

When I observed that I had used Riedel glassware for many years in my house for both formal and informal dining, and, just as importantly, for all the never-ending tastings for my books and articles, the National Wine Show committee immediately accepted my recommendation that the Show should use Riedel glasses. The long-serving head of Riedel in Australia, Mark Baulderstone, did not hesitate to make the glasses available at or near cost. He immediately understood the implications for the world of wine in Australia, and so it proved. A domino effect saw the same or similar glasses

Tastings reach a crescendo in February each year, here four tastings of 120 wines each await me.

adopted by all capital city and major regional wine shows across the country.

Sooner or later every new entrant to the wine arena became aware of the fundamental importance of appropriate glasses in a home or restaurant, extending to the various shapes and sizes for each type (and even age) of wine. I limited myself to eight: sparkling, riesling, semillon, chardonnay and pinot noir, shiraz, cabernet sauvignon, sweet wine, and fortified wines. For logistical reasons, it is impossible for wine shows to go past three glasses (sparkling, table wine and fortified), but the overall impact is massive.

Every now and then I (and my many peers) come up against the ISO glasses we abandoned years ago; I describe these glasses as little prisons, robbing the wine of its soul, its aroma, its texture and its structure. Pinot noir suffers more than any other variety, but that is scant comfort for the other wines being similarly maltreated. If you put an ISO (or worse, the thick glasses in a small bowl shape found in cheap restaurants) next to a Riedel, and taste the same wine out of each glass, it will be hard to believe that the wine is in fact the same.

As time has inexorably eroded my tasting stamina, I have developed a series of defensive measures. Long ago I learnt that a small nibble of a firm green olive helped strip the tannin build-up caused by tasting (say) 50 shirazs or cabernets in a row. A nibble of cheese ameliorated acid build-up from tasting a similar number of rieslings, semillons, sauvignon blancs and so forth.

Judging in South Africa introduced me to the concept of alternating white and red classes. This was entirely alien to the Australian practice since time immemorial of starting the day with sparkling or light-bodied white wines, then full-bodied white wines, next rosé, then light-bodied red wines such as pinot noir, then medium-bodied red wines, onto full-bodied red wines (there used to be a distinction between full-bodied soft finish, typically shiraz, and full-bodied firm finish, typically cabernet sauvignon), and finishing the day with fortified wines.

It had its logic, and when in the first half of the first year of the new millennium I drew up the daily roster rotating white and red classes, I made sure the panel chair could reorganise the classes in the traditional way with a minimum of disruption. Two other changes were made around this time. The massive classes of shiraz and chardonnay (200+) were subdivided into three equal groups (50–70) between three panels, each putting its gold medals elect into a final phase of (say) 10–15 wines that would be re-judged by the three panel chairs. Their responsibility was to choose the top gold medal, and confirm (gold) or relegate (to silver) the other wines.

This added a further complication of ensuring that the three panels finished their assessment at much the same time; this was not always easy. These split classes to one side, I also endeavoured to place the classes with 50 or more wines in the morning, while palates and minds were at their sharpest, leaving the smaller classes for the afternoon.

The responsibility of the Show Chair was to give advice when called upon by a panel chair at the conclusion of each class, either to give his/her opinion where the judges were divided, or where they were uncertain which of the gold medals was the best. Some panels would, as a matter of courtesy, finalise their discussions and simply invite the Chair to taste the top wines. Others simply got on with the next class. In this case, I would quietly ask the stewards to bring the glasses of the gold medals to my desk and make notes (for ultimate use in articles or books).

CHAPTER 13

THE FLIGHT OF ICARUS
1985–2010

It seems incredible that in the year Suzanne and I started Coldstream
Hills – an event that seems like yesterday – Australia imported more
wine (by value) than it exported. That said, events moved quickly
thereafter. In 1984 a group of English Masters of Wine had come
to Australia – and discovered an array of wines that were unknown
in the UK market. Prior to that visit, the general appreciation of
Australian red wines was of cooked, dull, brown offerings that did
not even attempt to show varietal character, and that were typically
labelled 'claret' or 'burgundy'. White wines were even less understood, which was not surprising given that most were called 'riesling',

OPPOSITE: *The author and wife Suzanne at the dedication of the
James Halliday Cellar 2010.*

but made from any variety which could be shoe-horned into a non-wooded style (dry or off-dry).

It was an image forged in the 1950s and 1960s, and was not far from the truth for cheap wines. But the 1970s had seen the moves towards cool regions; the first vintages of chardonnay; the rapid spread of cabernet sauvignon; the proliferation of small, family-owned wineries; and the realisation that the grapes from 100-year-old shiraz vines were more valuable for table wine than for fortified wine.

These changes were accelerating in the 1980s, and the MWs were, to put it mildly, impressed. As they headed home, they admonished us for not paying more attention to shiraz, accurately observing that familiarity had bred contempt. They were also enthusiastic about the new-generation riesling (then called rhine riesling to distinguish it from generic riesling style), semillon from the Hunter Valley, and chardonnay.

Winemakers readied themselves for the expected flood of orders for shiraz, semillon and riesling; instead orders came for cabernet sauvignon and chardonnay, varieties with international status. It was one thing for the MW gate-keepers to be convinced; another for English patrons of liquor stores, small or large, to change habits, to step into the unknown.

Within a couple of years, I was in London, talking to retailers and sommeliers. It immediately became clear that customers had had difficulty understanding wines which had such generosity, such abundant fruit flavours, and that were so different from the lean, often sulphurous or worse, offerings from French co-operatives at the same price.

Initial resistance overcome, English drinkers embraced the idea of these 'sunshine in a bottle' wines. They were helped by the pint-sized Hazel Murphy, who had jumped ship from the safety net of the far larger Australian Trade Office to establish the Australian Wine Bureau in 1985. With no budget to speak of, the one thing she was able to access without cost was Australian wine, and this provided all she needed for a 'glass in the hand' promotion. In less than a decade she poured Australian wine for 250,000 people in venues ranging from food and wine exhibitions to sporting events. In the 18 years before her departure from the Bureau in 2003, British consumption of Australian wine increased from next to nothing to 750,000 bottles a day. Pint-sized she may have been, but her energy and commitment were boundless, and were ultimately recognised by her receiving the Maurice O'Shea Award for Outstanding Contribution to the Australian Wine Industry (1996), and being made a Member of the Order of Australia (2004).

The Oatley family, supported by the marketing skills of Chris Hancock, were among the early movers to take up the challenge, making Rosemount Estate one of the best-known brands on the market. Almost overnight, the annual London Wine Trade Fair became an obligatory event for Australian producers. Unlike their Californian and European counterparts, who were largely represented by their UK distributors and sales representatives, the Australian owner/winemakers attended in person. The nerve centre for Australia, a general information bureau presided over by Hazel Murphy, also had liberal quantities of Coopers Pale Ale available at the end of each day.

The US market was far more fragmented, and thus was a very different proposition. One major initiative, involving several dozen small wineries (including Coldstream Hills) and partly sponsored by ACI, swept through major markets from New York to Florida at the end of the 1980s. But most of the work was done by the major wine producers, and with notable success.

The Chernobyl disaster in Ukraine in April 1986 caused the Swedish buying monopoly Systembolaget to look outside Europe for wine guaranteed to be free of radioactive fallout. Overnight, Sweden became a major market for Australia, the only downside being the requirement for a significant portion of sales to be in bulk and bottled in Sweden. (There were concerns about the possible blending of lesser wines of unknown origin.)

The two monopoly buyers of Canada, based in Ontario and Vancouver, also became large customers, and not just for a time. That of Vancouver was, and remains, one of the largest single buyers of wine in the world, and Canada became Australia's third-largest export destination after the UK and the US, although that was strongly challenged by China by late 2011. Indeed, if Hong Kong's imports of Australian wines were aggregated with China's, these two have now moved into third place.

The volume and value of exports doubled, then doubled again. A major marketing conference was convened to project likely growth over the next five years, and it grossly underestimated that growth. In 1990 another five-year plan was formulated, and again it underestimated growth: by 1995, value had grown to $386 million, compared with $8.6 million 10 years earlier.

Len Evans entered the fray. 'There is no point in five-year plans. This is not communist China. You must look beyond the short term to the long term. Why not the 30 years, to 2025?' And so, with funds donated by the Australian Wine Foundation (itself a creation of Len's, using Wolf Blass's money – Wolf the person, not the eponymous winery), a committee was established to formulate a vision for

FOLLOWING PAGES: *The amphitheatre in autumn, photo taken from the main office complex at Coldstream Hills.*

A Life in Wine

the 30 years through to 2025, covering both domestic and export markets. My role on that committee was to evaluate Australia's competitiveness in comparison with that of the other significant wine-exporting countries.

An elegant, deceptively small (12-page) report entitled 'Strategy 2025' was produced in full colour, using photographs, charts and easy-to-read tables to convey its vision 'that by the year 2025 the Australian wine industry will achieve $4.5 billion in annual sales by being the world's most influential and profitable supplier of branded wines'. Despite the lofty ambitions of the vision, the document was hailed by other Australian industries, and by some other wine-producing countries, as a remarkable accomplishment.

The $4.5 billion figure assumed annual domestic sales of $2 billion and export sales of $2.5 billion, made possible by an increase in vineyard area of 40,000 hectares by 2025, and a doubling of annual grape production from 850,000 tonnes to 1,650,000 tonnes by the same date. Neither friend nor foe could have imagined what would in fact follow.

Vineyard plantings grew by 80,000 hectares from the 1996 figure of 77,700 hectares to 158,000 hectares in 2002. In other words, double the target in six years, not 30 years. The sales target of $4.5 billion was achieved in 2003, 22 years early, with exports of $2.42 billion and domestic sales of $2.09 billion.

If it all seemed to be too good to be true, it was. On the domestic front, growers of chardonnay in the Murray Darling (Riverland) and Murrumbidgee (Riverina) regions

were receiving prices per tonne many times the cost of production. On the international front, a relatively weak Australian dollar resulted in irresistible value for money. Instead of capturing an 11 per cent market share in the UK by 2025, Australia claimed top spot in 2000. It retained that rank through to June 2010, with 21.1 per cent (by value), followed by the US (14.7 per cent), France (14 per cent) and Italy (13 per cent).

South Africa was still emerging from its forced hibernation during the apartheid sanction years; Chile was focused on the US; the south of France was still cosseted by EU subsidies and distillation; Italian exporters could not agree on generic campaigns; and California, with the noted exception of Gallo, was content to sell most of its wine in the US and Canada.

From the second half of the 1980s, ever-increasing droves of young Australian winemakers travelled to Europe to work as cellar hands in places as far-flung as Georgia, Hungary and Portugal, but mainly in France, Italy and (later) Spain. These Flying Winemakers (as they became known) needed to do no more than maintain strict hygiene and protection against oxidation to show how it was possible to make far better wine than hitherto achieved in the wineries in which they worked.

The all-powerful English supermarkets soon insisted on Australian winemakers being put in charge of parcels of wine being sold to them by the French and Italian co-operatives. To add insult to injury, French chardonnay from a Languedoc co-operative sold in England was labelled with the words 'Made in the Australian fashion'.

By 2003 Australia was the fourth-largest exporter (by value) in the world, closing the gap between it and Spain in third place, and with France and Italy a long way ahead (rather less if you did not treat sales between EU countries as exports). Then Australia had three record vintages in a row: 2004, 2005 and 2006. Moreover, they were high-quality vintages. It's a strange agricultural industry that recoils from a record crop of high-quality produce, but that is what happened.

Quite suddenly, the seemingly unstoppable export juggernaut slowed down, then went into reverse: the high point of export volume (787 million litres) and value ($2.9 billion) came in 2006/07. Since that time both volume and value have decreased year on year, volume to 366 million litres and value to $1.6 billion in the year to September 2011.

Grape and wine surpluses hurt growers and winemakers alike. Prices for uncontracted Riverland chardonnay plummeted to below the cost of production in 2010, and wine exports in bulk soared, at an average price of less than $1 per litre.

And if this were not enough, prolonged drought in the catchment of the Murray Darling had brought the system to the point of collapse, and prices for irrigation water increased significantly. The threat of nature was compounded by the fear of a change in the tax on wine:

instead of being calculated on its wholesale sales value, the Henry Review (officially *Australia's Future Tax System Review*) recommended a volumetric tax based on volume and alcohol. This would have led to a significant increase in the price of casks and cheap bottled wine, almost all coming from the Riverland and Riverina, and a lesser decrease in the price of high-quality bottled wine. The federal government responded by saying that there would be no change for the time being, but the threat remained very real.

All droughts end in floods, in this instance massive floods from nine months of rainfall across most of eastern Australia. The 2011 vintage was extremely difficult, impacting most on red wines, but, paradoxically, doing nothing to reduce the excess supply and resultant wine lake.

As it moved into the second decade of the 21st century, Australia had to make a decision: would it jump, or would it wait to be pushed? It had become increasingly obvious that the competition offered by Europe, South America, South Africa and California (in the guise of Gallo) was too great for Australia's basic wines (largely sourced from the Riverland and Riverina). Cheap labour (far less costly than that in Australia), plus increased quality, EU subsidies, and the buying power of the English supermarket chains combined to place intolerable pressure on margins.

Thus if Australia waited to be pushed out of the UK market for wines priced at £8 or less, it would lose both market share and the last shred of profit. If it jumped – as

Constellation did – it would have to find new markets for diminished production of basic wines, and increase its sales of quality wine. As at the start of 2010 the one realistic hope for increased wine export sales was Asia, headed by China, but also extending from India in the west to Taiwan and Korea in the east. Even here, competition would be substantial, notwithstanding Australia's market share in China of 20 per cent, behind France with 44 per cent, but in front of Chile, South Africa and California, with 8 per cent each.

Then, in June 2010, Wine Australia announced a multimillion-dollar push into China, backed by a dramatic prediction that China would become Australia's largest market by 2015. I had previously said on numerous occasions that at some point over the years to 2025 or 2030 China would become our largest market, and that it and its Asian neighbours would absorb the world wine surplus. I have to admit that I did not contemplate such a rapid development of the Chinese market.

Wine Australia's prediction was in part based on an expected 50 per cent increase in Australian exports to China in the 2010 calendar year, and in part on the opening of Wine Australia offices in Beijing, Shanghai and Hong Kong.

It was a highly volatile situation at the end of 2010. The ongoing effects of the Global Financial Crisis and the strong Australian dollar made it very difficult to generate even the slimmest of profit margins in the UK for any wine selling for less than £6, and it is in this sector that much of Australia's exports were placed. Nor was there any light at the end of the tunnel.

The US market was in slightly better shape, but the Australian 'little critter' honeymoon was over, period, full stop. A significant improvement in the US economy, based on falling unemployment and increased consumer spending on discretionary items, seemed a long way off, and there was intense competition for shelf space in shops, for wine lists in restaurants, and for online sales.

Canada, third after the UK and the US, offered more obvious opportunities, albeit on a smaller scale. But the elephant in the room was China.

Australia already dominated the all-important $15 to $20 sector in China, its share 80 per cent greater than that of France. By August 2011 Australia was exporting more bottles selling (ex Australia) for $10 or above to China than to any other market. This reflected the promotion of the 'A+' wines, itself a blueprint for exports into other markets. The upside remains impossible to quantify, with timing and volume the key imponderables. But it is with Asia that Australia's wine fortunes will rest.

In the meantime, it had become clear to informed observers that Australia had not devoted the time, energy and money necessary to increase domestic sales of A+ wines selling for over $20 a bottle. Coles' and Woolworths' dominance of the under $20 market was already unchallenged, and that share will remorselessly increase.

The A+ wines will have to be sold through independent liquor stores, restaurants, cellar doors, and (increasingly) online. Paradoxically, this will increase choice for educated consumers, and decrease prices for budget-conscious drinkers of everyday wine.

CHAPTER 14

THE LEN EVANS
MEMORIAL TUTORIALS

I have no doubt whatsoever that the Tutorials were regarded by Len as his crowning achievement. He derived no income from them; rather, the reverse. The tutorials in no way increased his profile outside the circle that knew what he had long given to the industry he loved. They were made possible because – with three major exceptions – he unashamedly called in debts and favours as he 'persuaded' 12 wine businesses intimately involved in the world of fine wine (mainly wineries) to become sponsors, at an annual cost of $6000 each.

The exceptions were first and foremost Basil Sellers, who endowed the Trust (the legal framework for the initiative) with $500,000 to be drawn down at $50,000 per annum; Qantas, which for 10 years (though no longer) provided two business-class tickets

---

OPPOSITE: *Like any gentleman, Len Evans tied his own bowtie*

Each year the Tutorial scholars purchased an adornment for the putting golf course at Tower Lodge. This, from the 2009 scholars, was one of the best.

to Europe for the Dux of each Tutorial; and Aubert de Villaine of the Domaine de la Romanée-Conti, who made two dozen bottles of DRC available each year at a special price – these would in due course provide revenue as well as the concluding tasting of each Tutorial. Then there have been numerous donations of wine, and some of cash, in the latter category with the Royal Sydney Wine Show to the fore. Somewhat uncharacteristically, Len decided (for no obvious reason) to reduce the prime sponsorship from $6000 to $5000 per annum.

The Tutorial is administered by Trustees through a slightly complex structure that makes donations tax-deductible. Far more important is the vision Len had for it, and which the Trustees are, hopefully, maintaining. Throughout his life, Len never stopped driving the messages that good is not good enough; that there should be no room for complacency; and that only by understanding the greatest wines of the Old World and New World alike could the opinion makers of the current generation pass on that knowledge to the next.

E ach year, the difficulty of obtaining appropriate wines for the five days of tastings for each tutorial increases. The greatest wines of France, in particular, will become ever more expensive. There has never previously been a 35-year period of unbroken price rises for the classed growth Bordeauxs, the grand and premier crus of Burgundy, the icon wines of the Northern Rhône Valley – the list goes on.

There are a number of reasons why this will become an increasingly acute problem, all deriving from the law of supply and demand. In the 800 years leading up to 1945, wine trade in Europe focused on domestic markets, with a limited number of extremely wealthy purchasers (originally royalty) buying much of the wine, and the sole export market of any significance being England.

The tentative entry of US buyers in the 1950s and 1960s, the even more tentative and disastrously timed entry of the Japanese into the en primeur market for the woeful 1972 vintage in Bordeaux, and the recession of 1974/75 led to the most precipitous decline in prices since the Depression. Then followed a string of very good to great vintages in the 1980s, the Robert Parker phenomenon, a rash of investment into Bordeaux leading to new winery facilities, new oak, infinitely more care of the vineyards and the appearance of second, and even third, labels.

As the Soviet Union crumbled and the oligarchs prospered, as both North and South America 'discovered' great wine and the investment potential it offered, as the greater Asian markets began to open up, initially through small windows offered by Singapore and Hong Kong, and at a feverish rate in the new millennium, and as the Chinese miracle made the achievements of Japan after World War II pale in comparison, demand has grown exponentially.

Because of the appellation controlée system, supply cannot increase to any measurable degree. It is true that a limited number of winemakers have followed Le Pin, a Pomerol garagiste, whose success shook the pillars of the establishment to their foundations. But even if there were a dozen Le Pins – or 50, or even 100 – it would make little difference given Le Pin's production of 350 cases a year – a number that increases its allure, of course.

It is also true that the wealth waiting to be harvested in good or bad vintages alike has brought moribund classified growths out of their slumber, leading to an incremental increase on the supply side. But it cannot balance demand.

Burgundy is in a different situation. The properties are much smaller, most are owner-occupied (vastly different from Bordeaux), and members of the family spend much of the year tending their vines, with little interest in promoting the wines – they leave that to the lucky few who have distribution rights. With the notable exception of Guigal, and the other producers in its ownership net, the same is true of the great producers of the Rhône Valley. But this does not alter the impact of demand; it only alters how it is managed (deflected may be a better word).

Italy is the first safety valve. While it was left to Angelo Gaja to blitz New York and establish a price hierarchy for Barolo that scales the heights, and to the industry and vision of various branches of the Antinori family to reinvent Tuscany, the momentum Italy has gained will feed on itself. Spain is today where Italy was 20 years ago, with its future already written in stone. These countries will not take market share from Fortress France: there is every possibility that they will simply be stepping stones for the new entrants into the global wine market as they seek to scale the vinous equivalents of Mount Everest.

For the time being, the great rieslings of Germany, Alsace and Austria (there joined by gruner veltliner) remain the bridesmaids. The German domestic market doesn't want to drink German riesling (the reasons for which are long and complicated), so all the top German riesling producers are forced to export a large proportion of their production, and their sheer quality and the cost of their production remain inadequately reflected in the prices they bring – they are underpriced, measured both against their cost of production and against their quality.

Particularly when it comes to the Mosel, some of us (led by me) would say long may it remain so.

When it comes to the classic wines of Australia – the true classics – the situation is in some ways equally dire. The great red wines of Maurice O'Shea, Colin Preece, Roger Warren and their contemporaries were typically made in quantities of 500 dozen or less. So were one-off gems like 1955 Wynns Michael Hermitage, 1965 Lindemans Bin 3100 and 3110 Hermitage, Woodleys Coonawarra Treasure Chest, 1954 and 1965 Tulloch Private Bin Hermitage – and so on. Only Grange remains procurable through the auction system, with occasional bottles of 1962 Bin 60A turning up – perhaps Schubert's greatest achievement. Down the track, screwcaps hold the promise of great 20 to 30-year-old semillons, rieslings and chardonnays, pinot noirs probably, and selected medium- to full-bodied reds certainly.

It is against this background that 12 scholars are selected each year from over 100 applicants to attend the five days of intensive tastings of the great wines of France, Australia, Spain, Italy, California, New Zealand and a few others. Selection of the applicants is necessarily a finely balanced exercise: the scholars must have a background knowledge of France's regions and appellation controlée systems; they must have done some wine show judging or equivalent blind tastings; and they must have demonstrated some overall ability in their chosen field of activity. Winemakers, sommeliers, wholesalers/

retailers, and journalists are the most represented, though there have been one or two amateurs (wine lovers) over the years.

The original focus was to identify outstanding palates, and fast-track their entry into serious wine show judging: the top five scholars each November were given positions as associates at the Royal Sydney Wine Show the following February, and are expected to go on from there. So successful has the Tutorial been that the pool of top-class judges overflows from time to time, and the desired outcome has shifted to its purest aim of awakening an awareness of the past, present and future of great wine.

Four of the most important sessions are half-day judgings of 30 chardonnays, 30 pinot noirs, 30 shirazs and 30 cabernets – shiraz viognier and Bordeaux blends falling within the purview of the latter two. The scholars are told the age of the youngest wine and that of the oldest (the wines are arranged in vintage order), but no more. They assume that there are a number of countries (and more regions) represented, but which countries and how many wines from each is in fact irrelevant, for the purpose of these four tastings is strictly to focus on the innate quality of each wine, not to guess its provenance.

The 'tutors' (Brian Croser, Ian McKenzie, Iain Riggs and myself, with Gary Steel and the local Hunter Valley winemaker who helped with the logistics of the selection co-opted) have in the meantime tasted the wines, and retired to come up with an agreed point score. Ian McKenzie, Brian Croser and I will know nothing about the wines, Iain Riggs and the organiser rather more, but we reach our conclusion by discussion, and without knowledge of the identity of the wine.

If a scholar's points are more than one point higher or lower than our agreed points, it will usually give rise to a penalty (unbeknownst to the scholar at that stage). Four or five will be asked to explain the reasons for their points, and only then will the identity of the wine (by ringmaster Iain Riggs), and the tutors' points, be revealed. However, there will be no further discussion on that wine.

Over the years the evaluation process has been refined: we look at the number of gold medals (18.5 points or above) awarded by each scholar; what number of those golds matched the points of the tutors; and how many gold medals were missed by the scholar. We also quickly identify those who favour the 'safety net' of 17.5 or 18 points, betting that few wines will score less than 16.5 or more than 19 points.

The afternoons are conventional masterclasses, albeit sometimes with a twist, but not blind tasting. Champagne, rieslings of the world, Burgundy and Bordeaux share the limelight – the champagne masterclass is timed to conclude as the Melbourne Cup is about to run.

The evenings are given over to variations of the Options Game, devised in the first instance by Len in the mid-1960s. He had the divine right to change the rules of the game whenever and in whatever manner he deemed fit. Thus there might, for example, be five glasses of red wine in front of each person. As a preamble, the scholars might be asked how many things they have in common, and what they are.

If the wines turned out to be the five first-growth wines of Bordeaux from the '82 vintage, the answer would be four: country, region, growth and vintage (variations in percentages of cabernet sauvignon, merlot, etc, ruling the variety question out of play). Having got to that point, the scholars would have to nominate the vintage, and the order in which the wines were placed – a total of 10 possible points.

Burgundy masterclass at the Len Evans Tutorial.

Other groups of wines might yield up to 15 points, though normally less, and single-wine options the usual five points. Given the overriding requirement that the wines be of high quality, there weren't too many oddities, but you never knew whether a stand-alone options wine might be a single DRC wine, a 100-year-old sauternes, or the occasional curve ball such as a 60-year-old Rioja. In the course of each night, there would be over 20 different wines.

The grand finale on Friday morning is the six DRC red burgundies: Echézeaux, Grands Echézeaux, Romanée St Vivant, Richebourg, La Tâche and Romanée-Conti, the latter two owned exclusively by DRC, and being the two greatest burgundies – and, for me, the two greatest wines – in the world. In the early days there were various vintages, which made the tasting fiendishly difficult. Most of the scholars come to the Tutorial never having tasted more than the occasional DRC, and certainly not Romanée-Conti itself.

These days there is a single vintage, theoretically making the tasting easier. Only one scholar has ever scored really well – Tom Carson (Chair of the Canberra National Wine Show, and distinguished winemaker for Yering Station, thereafter Yabby Lake), and that was in the days of mixed vintages. Two vintages at Coldstream Hills gave him a head start (my personal cellar used to be quite rich in DRCs), but it was no accident. He has the best palate of all judges and winemakers currently on the scene (and hence is Chair of the Canberra National Wine Show); only Jim Chatto (another star from the Tutorial, currently chief winemaker Pepper Tree Wines in the Hunter Valley) goes anywhere near close.

During the five days, the scholars stay in the luxury of Tower Estate, and all meals are staged there. The dollar value for each scholar selected for the Tutorial was calculated to be $7500 in 2010, and will outstrip indexation in the coming years. It is my fervent hope that the Tutorial will continue long into the future, with today's scholars tomorrow's tutors and Trustees. I have been told that it's 'the most exclusive wine school in the world'.

A Life in Wine

CHAPTER 15

THE SINGLE BOTTLE CLUB DINNERS: A REPRISE

On the way through the often-interrupted and not always sequential account of the development of the Australian wine industry and of my personal wine odyssey over the same period, I have touched on the highlights of some of the Single Bottle Club Dinners since the first dinner in 1977.

While they have been held every year – once or twice with two in a year – I have had to omit some, and limit my commentary on the remainder. Up to 2010, there had been 35 dinners, and it would be easy to write 1200 words on each (as I have in fact done for a number of dinners, and had published in the *Gourmet Traveller:*

OPPOSITE: *Pouring wines at a dinner held in 2010 at the Rockpool Restaurant, Sydney.*

Wine magazine). Each dinner, viewed in isolation, had a surfeit of rare and expensive wines, but over 40,000 words on dinner after dinner would cause acute literary indigestion.

Over the years, I have provided more wines than any other single member of the Club, and my cellar is no longer the treasure trove it once was. I have also provided many irreplaceable bottles for other tables in Melbourne, and each vintage at Coldstream Hills between 1988 and 1996 in particular further depleted my supply.

When asked, as I often am, how I could take such a cavalier attitude to wines such as these, I have several answers. First, it costs me nothing to take a bottle from my cellar. Second, the ultimate pleasure from a truly great bottle is to share it with your peers, and be part of the discussion that follows. Far better, surely, than to drink it on your own, and listen to the sound of one hand clapping. Finally, and most prosaically, better I get to share it, rather than some other so-and-so after my ashes have been scattered on House Block chardonnay.

But all is not lost. On the one hand, there are several thousands of bottles steadily deteriorating because they have cork closures. The majority are – or were – good wines I accumulated over the years, purchased with the intention of drinking them over decades to come. I still fully intend to continue the sporadic clean-outs, when I take car loads of old Australian wines down to the winery, where they either go straight to the tip or are shared by the winery team on the basis that they cost nothing, and some may have defied the cork gods and prove drinkable.

On the other hand, I do have a comfortable buffer of the wines I most enjoy: red Burgundies and Rhônes, rieslings from all over the world, semillons from the Hunter Valley, and top-end cool-climate chardonnays – all except the Burgundies are increasingly sealed

Le Club Dinner is spawned by the Single Bottle Club Dinners; this at Circa The Prince 2011, shows Saddle of Wild Shot Hare.

with screwcaps. If I am allowed another decade of life, many of these white wines will be 20 years old, and a guaranteed pleasure to drink.

Which brings me to André Simon, who died in 1970 aged 93 with only two magnums of Bordeaux left. He had written an epitaph saying 'a man dies too young if he leaves any wine in his cellar'. What perfect timing, they say. I take the contrary view: that this was precisely why he died. I shall underwrite my immortality by having at least some great bottles left. I must confess to one note of sadness: I increasingly come across or read about wines with a magnificent future, and have to restrain myself from buying them.

And so back to the Single Bottle Club Dinners, arbitrarily passing by the second half of the 1990s, and picking up on the Dinners between 2000 and 2005.

The new millennium heralded Evans's 70th birthday, an event marked by three days of celebrations involving almost 100 people at various stages. Lifelong friends Michael and Daphne Broadbent and Hugh and Judy Johnson flew in from London, more recent friends David Doyle and Jim Parks from California.

There was an Imperial Dinner, every couple assigned a regal persona chosen by Evans, and required to attend dressed in appropriate regalia. Having originally toyed with the idea of giving Suzanne the role of Catherine the Great, Len decreed that we would attend as the King and I. Only Suzanne knew I had decided to part with such hair as I had remaining in the hour before dinner; she was appointed the Royal Shearer. It had the desired effect. Evans, in his time-honoured role of Napoleon Bonaparte, was consumed with laughter, and I found the wash-and-go convenience sufficiently compelling to retain it to this day. All the wines came in Imperials (six-bottle equivalents) procured by Len over several years.

During Saturday and Sunday the sporting facilities of Loggerheads provided croquet on the croquet lawn, tennis on the half-tennis court, golf on the four/five hole golf course, boules through gardens and around trees (there was no out-of-bounds rule), darts and quoits, all played by pairs dressed in Great Gatsby sporting clothes. Pairs could not involve real-life partners/spouses, and only one person in each pair could have recognised skill at the game in question.

Each day had been staged with a background of live music, a Tiger Moth flypast, and copious amounts of champagne (and food).

In his youth, Len had been a golf professional at Huntingdale Golf Course in England, and while he was always ready to explain the difference between a golf professional (earning a skimpy living) and a professional golfer (earning much more), he was a very accomplished player. The birthday golf competition was a stroke play event on Saturday, with the two pairs on the lowest scores playing the final

Len Evans had long cast himself in the role of Napoleon Bonaparte; his wife Trish was his Josephine. This was taken at his 70th birthday.

on Sunday. This created a dilemma: the totally unsporting pair of Evans and all-round athlete Virginia Beavan had by far the lowest score, the next lowest Evans and daughter Sally, then myself and an equally mature Betty Flowers, who had in her younger days obviously been a very good player.

While, by any measure, the Evans and Beavan pair should have been disqualified, it was his birthday. Eventually the large number of people involved in the discussion came up with a compromise. Three pairs would contest the final: Len and Virginia, Len and Sally, and Betty and myself. While I do remember many of the details, suffice it to say that Betty and I had the exquisite pleasure of winning.

Twenty-six of us had a Friday night prelude with the Single Bottle Club Dinner, which opened with two bottles each of '70, '64 and '59 Dom Perignon Oenoteque. The marked field mushroom character on one of the '59s led to a spirited interchange between a critical Michael Broadbent and an approving Hugh Johnson, the latter declaring a touch of mushroom in aged champagne is to be expected.

Next came a glass – a small one – of what the menu called La Surprise, accompanied by caviar on blinis. Its golden colour suggested an aged table wine, but the spritz in the mouth (not visible in the glass) and the off-dry flavours suggested something else. And indeed it was: a 1907 Charles Heidsieck champagne recently recovered from a ship sunk in the Baltic Sea on its way to the US. Its $5000 a bottle price, courtesy of Christie's, London, seemed very expensive at the time, but now pales into insignificance compared to the €30,000 paid in 2010 for each of several bottles of champagne recovered from an even older watery grave, the wines having been protected by the low temperature of the water.

The wines that followed included two bottles of '78 Le Montrachet of DRC, acquired at Christie's, London, shortly prior to the dinner (at considerable cost, of course).

The cost of the wine was in part justified by our belief that this was the greatest white burgundy we had ever tasted, and in part by the magnificence of the quartet of '78 DRCs that followed: Romanée St Vivant (awesome length); Grands Echézeaux (more intense and tangy with a touch of licorice); La Tâche (an utterly fantastic bouquet penetrating every corner of one's consciousness, the palate confronting in its power and intensity); and Romanée-Conti (an extra dimension of power and length over and above the others, and a grip and intensity that incorporates but soars above alcohol, extract and tannin).

Four more great Burgundies starting with '69 and '61 La Tache came next, then nine great Bordeauxs between '61 and '49. Chateau d'Yquem '83, '67 and '45 were followed by '54 and '34 Henriques and Henriques Malmseys and a magnificent 1795 Barbeito Terrantez.

It seemed impossible that the Single Bottle Club Dinner of the following year could compete by any yardstick with that which preceded it, but one wine rose to the challenge. The story started when I received the Christie's auction catalogue of 19 July 2001 and saw a double magnum of 1865 Chateau Lafite listed for sale. The great twin vintages of the pre-phylloxera era were 1864 and '65, and 1874 and '75. Having owned, over time, several bottles of 1864 Chateau Lafite and 1865 Chateau Kirwan, I knew how great these wines could be, and my heart skipped a beat.

Moreover, the provenance of the double magnum was impeccable. The bottle (and 11 of its fellows) had come from the icy cold cellars of the Earl of Rosebery, where it had lain undisturbed for almost 100 years. Undisturbed, except that the neck of the bottle had been rewaxed when Berry Bros & Rudd had visited the cellars in 1932. The Earl-ancestor who had purchased the Lafite (variously in bottle, magnum and double magnum) had tasted a bottle on its arrival and pronounced it undrinkable and to be left – as it was.

This double magnum was first sold by Christie's in 1967, when 102 years old. On 21 May 1975 it was resold by Sotheby's with a note including 'ullage one inch – exceptional'. It came back to Christie's in 2001, described in the auction catalogue as 'in perfect condition', a colour photograph attesting to the fact. The catalogue had an estimated price range of £12,000–18,000. I knew this was

LEFT: *Breaking the hard wax capsule of the 1865 double magnum of Chateau Lafite.*
RIGHT: *This photograph of the Christie's slip label was taken at the same time.*

unduly conservative, and discussed bidding tactics with Len, and with Anthony Hanson, a good friend and head of Christie's.

Len and I had agreed to bid £25,000, not a penny more. Anthony Hanson responded that on this basis there was no need to bid by telephone, nor find someone in the room to bid, as Christie's would automatically do so on our behalf. I subsequently learnt that all room bidders had dropped out, and all but one phone bidder likewise. The auction proceeded in £500 bidding steps, and fate had it that the opposing phone bidder bid £24,500, with our pre-determined final bid of £25,000 following. The gods smiled, the phone bidder dropped out, and the wine was ours.

I then rang Hanson to seek his views and assistance on having the bottle re-corked in advance of its trip to Australia. He strongly advised against it, saying there was no sign of seepage, and the level was still perfect. Moreover, Chateau Lafite would no longer re-cork bottles that were older than 1945 at the Chateau. In retrospect, I am profoundly grateful that I accepted his advice, for when it came to remove the wax and the cork, and decant the bottle, there was no doubt that the wax was very old, the cork likewise. I am also grateful that we purchased – and drank – the bottle before the Chinese mania for Chateau Lafite took hold. In November 2010 three bottles of 1869 Chateau Lafite (a lesser vintage, and single bottles to wit) sold for a little under $250,000 each. At the rate of exchange prevailing when we bought our double magnum in 2001, the cost was $72,000; as at November 2010 it would have had a value in excess of $1 million. Would we have nonetheless elected to drink it, throwing away $900,000 or so, not knowing whether it would be drinkable or the most expensive vinegar ever sold? For my part, there would have been no question: drink it.

Hypotheticals to one side, the bottle had been standing upright for almost a month before the dinner, and had been moved with the utmost care to the bench where I planned to decant it, using a technique I had learnt from Jacques Seysses at Domaine Dujac during the 1983 vintage.

The glass of the double magnum was so dark in colour (green black) that it was only just possible to see the level of the wine – at the base of the short neck of the bottle – and impossible to gauge the colour of the wine or the amount of sediment. The technique called for a length of clear silicone tube to be affixed to a glass rod, the bottom of the tube whatever distance above the bottom of the bottle you estimated to be above the sediment. With four decanters lined up, you lower the rod into the bottle, and suck on the outer end of the tube to commence the siphon. Because the tube is clear, you can immediately tell whether you are free of sediment. If clear, all is well, and you fill each decanter without interrupting the flow.

If there is initial sediment, you immediately abort the process, withdraw the rod, raise the level of the tube, and try again.

But before all this I had to remove the wax and endeavour to remove the cork. The black wax was so hard and thick that it had to be chipped away with a hammer, a heart-stopping process, but satisfactorily completed. The cork was a different matter. On the plus side was its supple texture, thanks to the impervious nature of the wax. On the downside was the irregular, bulbous nature of the neck of the hand-blown bottle, with a profile akin to that of a port bottle. I did not expect to remove it in one piece, and provided it did not break up entirely into small pieces, the decanting method made larger chunks irrelevant. (In fact it came out in two pieces thanks to its pliability.)

I had snuck a little taste as I started the siphon, and knew this was a long way from vinegar, and the deep, healthy colour was plain for all to see, bringing gasps from those crowding around to watch proceedings. The aroma, too, was palpable, adding to the tension. The suction stopped before the fourth decanter was completely full, so the rod was removed, and the tube lowered 2cm. A fifth decanter was on standby in case the wine was not clear, but it was, so the fourth decanter was filled, and the fifth received some before the suction was broken.

At this point an awful thought crossed my mind. What if there was no sediment? It could only mean the wine was much, much younger, a possibility too terrible to contemplate. Another centimetre down, and up came sediment, impressive and reassuring. So the decanters were brought to the table and the wine poured, filling the room with the scent of violets and vinous heaven. Not a word was spoken until we had all spent minutes savouring the bouquet and embarked on the first sips of a voyage of discovery that was to continue for upwards of an hour.

A Life in Wine

The colour was incredible, the deepest red I have ever witnessed in an aged wine. The bouquet was unbelievably profound and complex, the perfumed aromas and flavours ranging through talc, violets, blackberry, cassis, anise, spice and plum. The texture was marvellous, as was the structure, both built around fine-grained, lingering tannins, perfect acidity, and no volatility whatsoever.

Instead of fading in the glass as do many very old wines, this continued to evolve, and the discussion became even more animated as the contribution of malbec (plum and plum jam) became more evident. Prior to the arrival of phylloxera, malbec was almost as important as cabernet sauvignon.

There were 26 of us, and we drank many other good wines that night; only the menu and my tasting notes remind me what they were, with no need of repetition here – except, that is, for the superb vintage (not solera) madeiras that concluded the night: 1875 Henriques and Henriques Malvasia, 1863 Barbeito Boal, 1848 Henriques and Henriques Boal (utterly exquisite, the best of the five); 1847 Henriques and Henriques Boal; and 1834 Barbeito Malvasia.

The 2002 Dinner was unique. I had unwisely mentioned to Len that a Christie's catalogue for a forthcoming auction on 6 December 2001 had a lot, photographed on its cover, comprising the 70 vintages of Latour between 1920 and 1999 inclusive, missing only the '27, '30, '31 and '32 (plus four vintages from the '90s – '91, '92, '93 and '97 – which we sourced in Australia), all execrable years. He commanded me to bid for it, and so I did: we succeeded at a price of £13,000 which, with commission added, equalled an average price of $568 a bottle at the then rate of exchange. In the same week a 46-vintage collection of Penfolds Grange was sold in an Australian auction with an average price of $5000 a bottle. We knew who had paid too much (or too little), and were duly pleased with ourselves.

The wines arrived intact, and at the last moment Frederic Engerer, Latour's CEO, was persuaded by Gary Steel to send a bottle of the 2000, the first of several 'vintages of the century' that were to follow (notably '05 and '09). Len and I were left with the difficult problem of deciding how the wines should be grouped once the obvious decision of spreading the wines over two dinners and two lunches had been taken. The master plan was to serve the lesser vintages at each lunch, and the greater vintages at each dinner, the preponderance of the younger wines on the first day, and of the older wines on the second day. (Age and quality do not walk hand in hand.)

The terroir of Chateau Latour has generally been accepted as the best in Bordeaux, with its stratified mix of river pebbles, fractured pieces of rock, sand and clay. The soil structure is free-draining in times of heavy rain, but it retains moisture in dry periods. Thus it copes very well with very warm and dry vintages, and – relatively speaking – even better in wet vintages when its neighbours struggle. My personal take was that it is – in racing parlance – a mud-runner.

So I was not unduly worried about the wines selected for the first lunch at Blaxland's Barn on Saturday, 27 July. Mercifully, Len had come up with the idea of pouring micro-tastes of the 18 wines on a side table, so we could choose which wines we actually wished to drink.

The wines, arranged in vintage order, were '93, '91, '84, '74, '72, '69, '68, '65, '63, '56, '54, '44, '42, '41, '40, '39, '38 and '35. Some of the wines I had tasted before, but with the qualified exception of the first three, not for many years. The wines had got older, and I had

---

OPPOSITE: *Single Bottle Club Dinner after Len's death; never quite the same.*

　　　　　　　A Life in Wine

become wiser (or harder to please). Difficult though the wines were, those served at lunch the next day were, in the main, even more disappointing. For the record, they were '97, '94, '92, '87, '80, '79, '77, '76, '73, '58, '57, '51, '50, '46, '36, '33, '25 and '22.

The obvious question was why were the wines so miserable, and why were the older wines in the brackets so unattractive? Part of the answer is that since 1982 the goal posts have been significantly moved. That vintage was the best since 1961, and was rightly praised by Robert Parker Jr, resulting in a win–win result for Parker and the chateaux owners. Another change came with the arrival first of Professor Emile Peynaud and later Michel Rolland, consultants who taught proprietors and winemakers the advantages of clean wineries and ripe grapes, and how to achieve these.

Parker has been both vilified and praised for his influence; either way, many observers have missed the point. He has no technical knowledge; all he did was massively increase the demand from the US for the full-bodied wines from Bordeaux and the Rhône Valley, the richer and riper the better.

The first consequence was the initiation of the longest unbroken run of price rises in the history of Bordeaux. As these rises compounded, chateaux proprietors found themselves in the historically unusual position of having positive cash-flow and profits. This encouraged them to modernise their wineries, invest in newly developed, sophisticated equipment, and in new oak barrels and vats. More care was taken in the vineyards, with ruthless selection of the best bunches at harvest, supplemented with all manner of sorting tables. Further selection of the best wine in barrel led to more second (and even third) labels.

Regardless of whether the climate warms or cools, we shall never again see Chateau Latour or its like producing miserable wines like those from the '70s ('77, '74, '73, '72), the '60s ('68, '65, '63) and the '50s ('56, '51, '50). Since I have no desire to or expectation of ever tasting wines such as those again, I pass on to the wines presented at the dinners, the first on Saturday, 27 July at Tower Lodge (as was the dinner the following night).

The wines were '00, '99, '98, '96, '95, '90, '89, '88, '86, '85, '83, '82, '81, '78, '71, '67, '60, '37, '34, '24 and '23. Cork issues had disfigured a number of the lunch wines, but they were of little practical concern with these wines. The '00, '99, '96 and '90 were utterly glorious, however unready the first two in particular may have been. The one major disappointment was the '82; I have tasted many bottles of this wine, most superb, but some spoilt by distinct brettanomyces, as was this one.

All the reservations and disappointments disappeared with the dinner on Sunday night. Here I decided to present the first three flights of five wines in vintage order, but to extract what I hoped would be the greatest five wines in the final flight. Thus we started with the '75, '70 (a glorious bottle of an outstanding wine), '66, '64 and '62. Next came the second flight of '55 (totally brilliant), '53, '52, '49 (one of the greatest wines of the entire tasting, with almost unbelievable length and persistence of flavour) and '48.

The third flight started with '47, followed by '43 (justified in its reputation as the best wartime vintage, and indeed the best since '29), '26 (deeply coloured, hugely powerful and massively rich), '21 (exotically fragrant, hyper-rich and velvety) and '20 (oxidised and vinegary, thanks to the cork).

The last flight gave rise to superlative after superlative: '61, '59, '45, '29 and '28. The cork gods were in their most benevolent mood, and every wine lived up to or exceeded expectations. Michael Broadbent regards the '45 as a challenge to the great pre-phylloxera vintage of 1865, and our bottle of '45 showed why: superb colour, vibrant fruit aromas, an almost viscous, ultra-smooth entry into the mouth, then merging with perfectly weighted tannins on the back-palate and finish.

In his *Great Vintage Wine Book* Broadbent gave the '29 Chateau Latour his maximum five-star rating, adding 'One is tempted to add a sixth star.' I agreed, giving it 100 points as the greatest of greats, intensely aromatic, and sheer perfection in the mouth, its supple, silky texture and tannins providing exquisite harmony and balance, the length and persistence of the finish and aftertaste quite awesome.

The final wine, the '28, was a fitting finale. Deeper in colour than the '29, the bouquet had potent and classic cassis, cedar and cigar box aromas, the palate demonstrating the legendary strength of the wine. Monumental in every way, with immense power and huge tannins wrapped around the well of black fruits. Writing in 1990, Broadbent suggested that the wine had another half a century of life, and in 2002 that still seemed correct.

How do I reconcile these observations with my take on the wines served at the two lunches? Simply because the growing season conditions were perfect, and the yields low to very low.

The 2004 dinner, with founding member Hermann Schneider making his reappearance as guest chef, was marked by superbly cho-sen and executed food to accompany verticals of Clos de Mesnil, Marc Bredif Vouvray ('53, '47, '37, '33 and '28 from my cellar), Dr Barolet burgundies ('49, three '37s and '26), top end Bordeaux (two '61s, '59, '49 and '45), and Mosel Eisweins ('79, two '75s and two '71s). I hurry on because needs must, and because of the dinner that was to follow on 9 September 2005, celebrating Len's 75th birthday.

Planning had begun almost a year previously; unknown to Len, the wines were to celebrate the year of his conception (1929), as spectacular a vintage as the year of his birth (1930) was dismal. Serge Dansereau returned as chef – the only person to fill the role three times – notwithstanding that he was leaving for France two days later, and refusing to be paid, and with his two sous chefs coming at a cut-rate price.

There was always a surfeit of wine pourers coming from the pool of young Hunter winemakers, and this year competition was especially intense. All this was transpiring long before WikiLeaks, but I was very nervous that Len might ferret out the theme of the evening, and – worse still – learn of the vinous centrepiece. So my emails to all and sundry were full of admonishments not to discuss the planned wines with anyone outside those attending, death by stoning the penalty for anyone letting the secret out.

As we finally sat down for the dinner, I was seated directly opposite Len, and watched his face intently as he opened his menu. It was clear that there had been no leaks: his face, and a few strangled words of disbelieving thanks, said it all.

The aperitif champagnes were non-vintage, making their way onto the list because they have never been sold in Australia. They were three grand cru single-vineyard wines of Moet et Chandon: Les Vignes de Saran, 100 per cent chardonnay; Les Champs de Romont, 100 per cent pinot meunier; and Les Sarmants d'Ay, 100 per cent pinot noir. Lest it be thought the drinking of these was lèse majesté, they were followed by 1929 Bollinger, supplied ex-cellar, with all the richness and complexity unique to very old champagne, and unique to Bollinger and Krug. Lashings of caviar, raw tuna on cucumber, and anchovy feuilleté sticks were admirable foils.

A quartet of '71, '59, '55 and '29 Moulin Touchais came next, the juxtaposition of sweetness and high acidity always posing a challenge for the chef. Serge's answer was (as per the menu), Foie gras et sa marmalade de légumes tartine rôtie.

While there can be arguments about which of Bordeaux and Burgundy should be served first, there was no such debate this night. We started with the four '29 Bordeauxs; the foreplay over, we could move to the first bracket of '29 Burgundies, all recently moved from their respective cellars. Bouchard Père et Fils Beaune Teurons set the scene: deeply coloured, strikingly rich, sweet and potent, with strong tannins in support. A little too much of a good thing, perhaps, and not as classic as the following Seguin Manuel Aloxe Corton, which was very long, spicy, fine and elegant. Two more Seguin Manuel wines followed: the powerful and tight Clos St Denis had great texture, mouthfeel and length, making it one of the stars of the night; the Corton Marechaudes had a gloriously youthful colour presaging its voluminous flavours, set within a silky and supple mouthfeel.

Serge had chosen one of his signature dishes for this flight: Ravioli de ris de veau ragoût de champignon, sauce aux cêpes, lifting the tempo with Confit de canard boudin noir au choux for the next four '29 Burgundies. When the '03 vintage caught Burgundy with its heat, '29 was the year picked by winemakers as the nearest previous equivalent – although as some observers were quick to point out, no one who had made wine in 1929 was still making it in 2003.

Whatever, the Le Corton of Bouchard Père et Fils was exceptionally powerful, youthful and sweet with layered richness; you could not deny the link with the style of the best '03s. The Seguin Manuel Mazis Chambertin that followed was on another plane, its gloriously fragrant and spicy aromas promising the utterly beautiful and very long palate that followed. Patriarche Père et Fils, purchased direct from its cellars in Beaune earlier that year, came next, a curate's egg with a lovely mid-palate, but a faltering finish suggesting a little oxidation.

A Life in Wine

By good luck, Dufouluer Père et Fils' Chambertin was the last of the four wines: it was bursting with red cherries and plums on its silky, yet structured, palate. This negociant business still exists, but its current modest reputation underlines the absence of wines such as this.

So the great moment finally arrived, the magnum of Romanée-Conti purchased from a Belgian cellar almost a year earlier, after prolonged email interchanges, photos of the bottle provided and examined, and a low-key comment from Aubert de Villaine (of DRC) that '29 had been the best of a mammoth vertical tasting of Romanée-Contis staged by a Swiss collector not long previously. (Low-key, because I subsequently learnt that Aubert was worried about us paying too much for a bottle that may have not lived up to our expectations.)

He needn't have worried: still deep in colour, its profound, impossibly complex, aromas changed moment by moment, ever revealing a new facet of this vinous diamond. At its heart lay an unfathomable well of dark berry fruits and plums, the palate a lyrical combination of finesse and intensity. Parmagiana was on the table as a strictly optional extra.

We reluctantly moved on to an ethereal, graceful '29 Chateau Romer du Hayot and my last bottle of '21 Marc Bredif Vouvray Liquoreux, a wine paired several times with '21 Chateau d'Yquem, and never yielding. Glowing golden brown, it weaved ginger, brandy snap, lemon juice and cumquat in an ever-more intense embrace, its extreme length and balance a given. A great farewell for a great wine.

Three solera madeiras finished the night: 1822 Bual (Cossart Gordon), 1864 Grand Cama de Lobos (Blandys) and 1870 Bual (Camara Lomelino).

CHAPTER 16

FAREWELL

It is a statement of the obvious that my life has taken many twists and turns, some as a result of conscious decisions on my part, others chance outcomes of being in the right place at the right time.

My choice in 1988 to leave the substantial economic shelter provided by my partnership in Clayton Utz had major financial implications. A sharp intake of breath often accompanied my statement to audiences that in '88 I divorced my wife and married my mistress, before I explained that law had been my wife, wine my mistress, and collective breath exhaled. But I didn't explain that my only parting income from Clayton Utz was the progressive payment of the value of my unbilled work and a short-lived small pension. On the other side, I had agreed to forego any salary from Coldstream Hills until its profits before tax exceeded $300,000 a year (a figure not achieved for many years).

OPPOSITE: *The author, as ever, with a glass of wine in hand*

This left me without, as they say, visible means of support other than my income as a wine writer. Luckily, I had foreseen the day that I would face the problem, and had taken all the opportunities that came from being in the right places at the right times as a wine journalist and author. Thus every newspaper article, every magazine contribution, and every book I wrote was commissioned by the various publishers involved.

My first magazine articles were written for *Epicurean* magazine around 1970 at the request of its editor, and there has never been a time since that I have not written for at least one magazine (sometimes two or more) for every edition, and made numerous one-off contributions for magazines in Europe, the US and/or Asia.

Between 1978 and 1984 I wrote a weekly column for the (now defunct) *National Times*; since 1984 I have contributed a weekly column for *The Australian*. When I say I have never missed a deadline, newly arrived editors give me a glance of amused disbelief. In a quarter of a century, I have only had two meetings on content, although it is true that for a while my column was shifted from one day of the week to another, into and out of, and back into the *Australian Weekend Magazine*. At one glorious time, I had 1500 words a week, now shrunk to 350 (plus or minus a few words).

Since 1979 I have written or co-authored/contributed to 65 books, once again commissioned by various publishers. Some have been translated into Japanese, French, German, Danish, Icelandic and Polish.

Art & Science was awarded the 1993 James Beard Award and the Veuve Clicquot Award; the *Wine Atlas of California* was the Wine Spectator Book of the Year in 1994, and won the IACP/Julia Child Award for Best Wine, Spirits or Beer Book 1994. I was awarded the Wine Literary Award 2002 for Exceptional Contribution to the

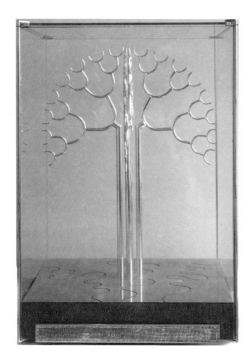

ABOVE LEFT: *The much cherished Maurice O'Shea Award (in solid silver)*
ABOVE RIGHT: *Julia Child Award for the Wine Atlas of California*
BELOW LEFT: *James Beard Award for the Art & Science of Wine*
BELOW RIGHT: *A magnum of 1938 Vintage Krug – quite a birthday present, intended for my 60th but in fact kept until my 70th, still superb (a gift from Krug).*

Literature of Wine (presented by the Wine Appreciation Guild of California). Along the way the *Wine Atlas of Australia* (2008 edition) was awarded the Louis Roederer Trophy for Best International Wine Book of the Year (London), and the 2006 edition of the *Wine Companion* won the Wine Communicator of the Year Award in 2005, having been published at the end of July 2005, albeit entitled 2006.

When international travel (6–12 times a year) and interstate travel (continuous throughout the year) is taken into account, along with over 50 days a year bench-tasting 120 wines a day for the *Companion* and other writing assignments, the question I am asked more than any other is 'How do you do it?'

Suzanne indirectly provided the answer when she caught me working on Christmas Day over 12 years ago and observed, 'You do realise you will have worked for 364½ days this year by New Year's Eve.' The outcome was an agreement to have at least one week's holiday away from wine. Thus we have been to Prague, the highlands of Bali, China, Madagascar, Turkey, Kangaroo Island, the Kimberley, Rajasthan, Vietnam and Cambodia, and on many occasions to game parks in South Africa. Some of these visits have been for two or more weeks, but I don't get any carried forward benefit – the clock starts again on 1 January each year.

Burgundy, where our house (jointly owned with others) is situated, and where we have spent each May, is a grey area, combining work and holiday on a day-to-day calendar.

The foregoing apart, I work seven days a week, for plus or minus 10 hours a day. I always work on planes, and get quite stressed if I run out of work on long-haul flights (unless, that is, I have a book or books that I have specially saved for the trip). I listen to ABC News Radio while shaving and showering in the morning, read *The*

ABOVE LEFT: *Celebrating the award of the Ian Mackey Trophy to the 1991 Coldstream Hills Pinot Noir for Best Wine Export from Australia in 1992.*

ABOVE RIGHT: *The author's induction as a Baron of the Barossa.*

Australian while I am having lunch in my home office, and watch the 7pm *ABC News* followed by *7.30* plus all international cricket and rugby union matches, and major golf and tennis tournaments. These also provide quality ironing time, as I live in an equal opportunity house when it comes to ironing.

So the next question is, 'Why do you do it?' or 'How do you do it?' or 'Do you enjoy the travel?' Well, as I have indicated, I do need to earn an income, which answers the 'why' question, and the 'how' is (I assume) apparent from above.

As to the last question, the answer is a qualified yes. Qualified, because (roughly speaking) between 10 December and 10 January each year I don't have to leap out of bed the second the alarm clock goes off trying to immediately remember how much time I have to get to the airport; whether or not I have organised my packing; and how many days will I be away for. Instead I can relax for a few minutes before heading to the bathroom and listening to the news on the radio.

So the clock is still ticking, the major restraints (or annoyances) being the steady erosion of my short-term memory (I'm assured I don't have early onset Alzheimer's) and a lexicon of operations in a two-page spreadsheet to staple to the hospital admission question: 'Have you previously had an operation; if so, when and for what?'

There was no previous year in my life as momentous as 2010, and it is inconceivable that any future year will go close to equalling it. But even though the events are fresh in my mind as I write these words, there is no way I can prioritise them, and a simple time chronology doesn't help.

The most unexpected event was being made Old Cranbrookian of the Year, as it came out of the blue with absolutely no warning. Indeed, when I travelled to Sydney to speak to the Cranbrook School assembly and attend several meetings, it was the first time I had stepped inside the gates for 55 years. Memories flooded back; while there were many new buildings, some – notably the dining room – were unchanged. And of course, there were some contemporaries – or near thereto – including my long-term friend Jack Friday, and Denis Lynch, a steward at the Sydney Royal Wine Show for much of the three decades that I judged there. I suspect these two played a key role in my nomination and the phone call from the headmaster, Jeremy Maiden, asking whether I was prepared to accept the honour, to which there was only one possible answer.

Over the years I had received a considerable number of envelopes with the crest of the federal Government House marked

'Honours-in-Confidence'. They contained letters seeking my views on the merits of a possible award to a person in the wine industry of an honour within the Order of Australia. So when I opened another envelope thus marked, I expected another request for my opinion on the merits of giving an award to someone or other.

Instead, it was a letter informing me that I was being considered as a recipient of an award, asking me whether I would accept it if offered, and making it abundantly clear that I was to inform no one of the fact that I might be recognised for my contribution to the industry as a winemaker, wine judge and author. I told Suzanne, but no one else, and waited for the publication of the awards on the Queen's Birthday, 14 June.

And so on that day I knew I was to be made a Member of the Order of Australia, entitled to append the letters AM after my name. The obvious question is whether I value this recognition more highly than the Maurice O'Shea award I received in 1995 for much the same contribution. The AM has a far broader recognition across society as a whole, but the O'Shea is better understood by those in the wine industry, and it is the one I treasure most.

On 1 October I travelled to the Hunter Valley to attend Brokenwood's 40th birthday celebrations. It was a three-day affair, and even though 27 years had elapsed since I had sold my share of it, many happy memories of those bygone years underlined the vicarious pride I have in its success and confidence in its future.

Eleven days later, back in the Yarra Valley, I was part of the 25th birthday celebrations of Coldstream Hills, although I'm not too sure how many people realised it was the anniversary. For it was the official opening of the new winery, built at a cost in excess of $5 million around the remaining parts of the original winery.

The author with David Dearie, CEO of Treasury Wine Estates, at the naming of the James Halliday Cellar.

It was the culmination of a process that dated back several years, and took tangible shape in 2009. Both before and after the '08 vintage it had become increasingly obvious that the winery that had been designed and built in time for the '88 vintage – with a capacity of 500 tonnes – could not safely or efficiently deal with an intake which had grown to 1300 to 1500 tonnes (depending on the vintage). Certainly, the barrel storage facilities have been progressively expanded, but the grape receival and processing areas had barely changed.

We (Coldstream Hills) had been one of several wineries within Foster's considered for upgrade, but had lost out to the winery-within-a-winery constructed at Wynns Coonawarra Estate to handle (relatively) small amounts of red grapes of the highest quality to make their iconic reds (John Riddoch Cabernet Sauvignon, Michael Shiraz and an upcoming series of limited-volume, single-vineyard wines). Chief winemaker Sue Hodder and viticulturist Allen Jenkins fully deserved the winery, and we felt no jealousy.

Then the '08 vintage came along, with generous yields of good-quality grapes; the problem was that every variety ripened with incredible speed and all at much the same time. We were deluged with pinot noir, but had no hope of fermenting more than a portion of the pinot in small open fermenters with whole bunches and pigeage. Much of it had to be treated much as if it were cabernet sauvignon: crushed and pumped to static closed fermenters. The resulting wine was technically sound and had varietal character, but was utterly inappropriate to the Coldstream Hills style. It was sold in bulk to another Yarra Valley producer for less than its cost of production, and for a fraction of the value it would have realised if used for and sold as Coldstream Hills Pinot Noir.

It immeasurably strengthened the financial case for the winery upgrade, but there were two problems. First, Foster's, in common with the other large wine producers, was battling with excess grape and wine production, and had placed a number of wineries, vineyards and brands on the market to slim down the asset values on their balance sheets. Why would it head in the opposite direction by increasing its investment in Coldstream Hills? Second, the GFC was creating economic chaos around the world, most obviously in Australia's two largest export markets, the UK and the US.

Against the odds, we knew that the re-make proposal was receiving serious attention, and with bated breath (unofficially) followed its progress through the labyrinthine pathways of the large corporation that Foster's was and is. Eventually, I became sufficiently encouraged to put a magnum of 1975 RD Bollinger in my office wine fridge, and announce to the winery team that it would be drunk if and when the day came that the proposal was formally approved.

That great day arrived, the Bollinger was duly consumed, and tenders went out for the construction of the winery (for it effectively meant a new winery built on and around the perimeters of the existing buildings) with a scheduled completion date prior to the 2010 vintage.

Unfortunately, the successful tenderer worked strictly to union rules, and the site foreman made it his personal mission to make things as difficult as possible for the winemaking team, and for the sub-contractor with the largest single responsibility: the fabrication and installation of the steel and stainless steel work (other than fermentation tanks, which were manufactured off-site). The sub-contractor wanted to work long hours, ignore high temperatures, and work weekends, but locked gates and union rules initially thwarted him ... until we worked out a way through the gates.

The result was a time-honoured one for new wineries: building works proceeding at full pace as vintage started. The site foreman had been fired, and his replacement was far more co-operative, but the early grape intake had to be fermented at Yarra Burn winery. As soon as it was possible to install open fermenters, they were filled, within hours, and blood pressures fell. It was lucky that as a consultant I had no executive role, for if I had, the initial foreman would have been throttled and I jailed for murder. The ever-calm Andrew Fleming and Foster's engineer Lawrie Mew simply and sensibly made the best of a bad situation, secure in the knowledge that the 2011 vintage would be carried out in the spacious purpose-designed winery.

As the opening day approached, I learnt that the winery would be officially named the James Halliday Cellar. The thought had never crossed my mind, and I was genuinely overwhelmed. Had I realised the pomp and circumstance of the unveiling of the plaque recording the day (and my name) my pleasure might have been thoroughly compromised (by anxiety and a wish not to be made a fuss of), but in the end the goodwill of the day meant my fears were groundless.

Whatever the future may hold for Coldstream Hills, I think the building of the new winery on the original site on top of the amphitheatre means it is unlikely that the brand and its physical assets will ever be broken up. As I said at the dedication ceremony, my ashes will be scattered on the House Block chardonnay, and I will rise from the dead to protect what I still regard as my baby if it is threatened with dismemberment.

My attitude to Coldstream Hills has been precisely the same since day one, when Suzanne and I owned 100 per cent of it, through 1988, when we owned 51 per cent, then 1993, by which time our share had fallen to around 23 per cent, and finally to 1996, when it fell to zero. Suzanne has accompanied me every day on this journey, and has worked tirelessly on our house since it became ours in 1996.

As I write these words, the 14-year drought has ended, the dams are all full, and the Yarra Valley has never been more beautifully green. My office in (or under) the house shares the sweeping views out over the Valley with the house proper, and the trees in the front are filled with birds. It is inhabited by myself and my two fiercely loyal and protective personal assistants, Paula Grey and Beth Anthony.

Do I have any regrets? Yes, a few, but so would anyone who has lived for 73 years. Would I change anything? No. Are there still mountains to climb? I hope so, particularly if they are not too large.

FOLLOWING PAGE: *A view I shall never tire of...*

ACKNOWLEDGEMENTS

It may seem strange, but I have found this difficult to write, with several drafts hitting the waste-paper basket.

The truth is that I have had extraordinary luck in finding my way to where I am today: I just happened to be in the right places at the right times. When I completed my BA LLB degrees at the University of Sydney in 1961, I thought my future was largely cut and dried – to practise as a solicitor for five or so years, and then head to the Bar.

Nothing could have been further from my mind than that by the end of that decade, I would have amassed a substantial wine cellar; met my mentor and life-long friend Len Evans; been asked to write a wine column; and embarked on the search for what would become Brokenwood.

Even then I did not contemplate a decision that I ultimately took in 1988 to divorce my wife (law) and marry my mistress (wine). In the intervening years I had written many books on wine, written countless newspaper and magazine articles, become a senior wine show judge, and travelled the world visiting its greatest wine regions, moved from Sydney to Melbourne for my law firm (having been its first managing partner) and with my wife Suzanne established Coldstream Hills in 1985.

Not once did I initiate a book or write a column off my own bat: in every case I was approached by the publisher. My wine show judging was initiated by Len Evans, and my overseas travels revolved around consultancy work for would-be Australian importers, speaking at conferences, promoting Coldstream Hills and (frequently) the cause of fine Australian wine.

I hope you will not see this as hubris, for I am simply seeking to explain how lucky I have been in this chronology. But even this leaves unsaid the privilege of being part of the wine community, of sharing great bottles with friends, sharing ideas with grape growers and winemakers (particularly the team at Coldstream Hills, headed by Andrew Fleming), wine judges and my peers in journalism.

My heartfelt thanks go to all those who have intersected with my life in wine, but there are some whom I must specially acknowledge and thank. First is my wife Suzanne who has always supported me, for better or worse. So, too, did Len Evans until the day he died; in the opening chapter I have written about our friendship, and the loss I still feel, and will continue to feel until my ashes are scattered on House Block chardonnay, 30 or so metres away as I write these words.

I have been extremely fortunate with my publishers: for over 20 years what is now called Harper Collins, and since 2006 Hardie Grant. Since day one, Sandy Grant has placed enormous faith in me, for which I am profoundly grateful. We have what is effectively an equal partnership (joint venture is the correct term) and it is one that will endure so long as I can pick up a pen. Yes, that curious relic of time gone by, but which I still use. With Sandy go his fellow directors, who clearly have similar faith in him.

Finally, there are the two warriors at the battlefront, my PAs. Paula Grey has been with me for 20 years, and Beth Anthony for 12 years. Beth has had primary responsibility for this book, Paula for the annual Wine Companion. We all occupy the same de facto open plan office under my house, and Paula and Beth have risen to the task of saving me from myself with great humour and infinite patience. I dread the thought of losing either of them.